DID CHRIST REALLY LIVE?

DID CHRIST REALLY LIVE?

BY

H. G. WOOD

Author of

The Truth and Error of Communism, Henry T.
Hodgkin, Christianity and the Nature of History, etc.

STUDENT CHRISTIAN MOVEMENT PRESS
58 BLOOMSBURY STREET, LONDON, W.C.1

First published July 1938

PRINTED IN GREAT BRITAIN BY
NORTHUMBERLAND PRESS LIMITED
GATESHEAD ON TYNE

To
BLIND LEADERS OF THE BLIND
IN THE HOPE THAT BOTH
MAY OPEN THEIR EYES

PREFACE

THE theories discussed in this book will probably be unfamiliar and bewildering to many readers. They may even wonder whether the Christ-myth idea is of sufficient general interest to warrant its inclusion among the publications of the Religious Book Club. But books in support of this strange theory are still being published and may be found on every bookstall. More young people than we often realize are troubled or misled by the suggestion that Jesus never lived. We cannot rightly ignore the subject. And revivals of interest in the Christ-myth are not unlikely. When I was in Chicago in 1931, I visited a Russian Workers' Club in which anti-religious posters were displayed. These included posters designed to equate Jesus with Mithras and Osiris. Certainly Christ-myth assumptions will appear in any Marxist anti-God campaign, and this book may serve as a kind of spiritual air raid precaution—a preservative against poison gas.

The method of treatment which I have adopted may make rather heavy demands on the attention of the reader, but I hope the effort involved will bring its reward. I have thought it best not to traverse all the stock arguments of Christ-myth theorists, but to examine in detail two propositions advanced by the late J. M. Robertson. If the discussion of the second proposition seems too detailed, the reader will catch the main drift of the argument, if he or she passes on from the end of Chapter V to Chapter IX, or even to Chapter X. But the weakness of Christ-myth theories is only apparent when they are treated seriously and in detail.

I have hesitated about choosing Mr. Robertson's theses for examination since he is no longer here to defend them. I trust that in a vigorous criticism I have said nothing disrespectful to the memory of one whose services to liberalism in thought and politics were very genuine. I have tried to safeguard myself by studiously understating the case against Mr. Robertson's views. It must be remembered that what the logicians call the *onus probandi*, the burden of proof, rests on advocates of the Christ-myth. We have not to advance reasons to prove that Jesus Christ is a historical character. They have to show that he never existed, and this they cannot do.

In Chapter XII I have included some paragraphs from a little book on *Rationalism and Historical Criticism*, which is now out of print.

H. G. Wood.

March 1st, 1938.

CONTENTS

9

Contents

CHAPTER I

To many readers the question which forms the title of this book may come as a surprise and even as something of a shock. Whatever our religious beliefs about him, most of us assume without question that Jesus belongs to history and we are amazed to learn that there are those who doubt whether he ever really lived. The very idea that Jesus should be relegated to the realm of fiction and myth may strike us as so fantastic, that we have not patience enough to examine it. Yet during the last hundred years quite a number of really able men have persuaded themselves that the figure of Jesus is the figment of pious imagination. A case that convinced so distinguished a literary critic as Georg Brandes cannot be altogether negligible, and once the question has been raised, we cannot rightly ignore it. We have no refuge but in truth, and if those who deny that Jesus Christ ever lived have reason and the weight of evidence on their side, the sooner we realize it the better. And if on investigation they turn out to be mistaken, we may hope to gain much for our knowledge of Jesus and for our understanding of religion and history.

11

If we plunge haphazard and unprepared into post-war critical studies of the beginnings of Christianity we may appreciate more sympathetically the reasons which have led some men to regard Christ as a myth. It is now generally recognized that the gospels are not biographies and do not enable us to write any detailed authoritative life of Christ. The gospels were written by believers to persuade others to believe. They are not essays in historical portraiture: they are essays in evangelism. This is as true of the earliest gospel, the gospel of Mark, as it is of the latest, the gospel of John. A recent and brilliant series of Bampton Lectures on "History and interpretation in the gospels" will leave on the mind of the ordinary reader the impression that even in Mark there is a great deal of interpretation and very little history. Is it then extravagant to suggest that there may be no history at all?

Many modern scholars tell us that we must go to the gospels to find out not so much what Jesus was as what the early Church thought he was or must have been. And the first generations of Christians did not come to Jesus with empty minds. They had ideas about the Messiah, ideas of what he would be and of what he ought to be. They ransacked the Old Testament for hints as to the nature and work of the promised deliverer of Israel. Undoubtedly this study of Old Testament prophecies has influenced the account they give of Jesus. Early Gentile converts were familiar with Lords many; they knew of religious societies united in devotion to a hero-God, Osiris it might be, or Adonis, or Mithras. Some had belonged to such societies and had partaken in the sacraments which linked the worshippers in fellowship with their Lord and with one another. Such Gentile converts thought of Jesus as Lord, and expected him to do for them, all and more than all that Osiris or Adonis or Mithras could do for their followers. Yet others, both Jews and Greeks, were more philosophically inclined. They had thought much about the Wisdom or Word of God—the Word that was in the beginning with God and whereby God made the world. They were familiar with the philosophic term, the Logos (= the Word), and knew what Plato and the Stoics taught concerning it. This Logos or Word might dwell with man, and might be incarnate in a man. But when men confessed their faith in Jesus as the Christ, or as Lord, or as the Word of God incarnate, they readily believed and perhaps readily invented stories about him which supported or expressed their faith. What was to prevent them attributing to Jesus anything which seemed to them appropriate? If critics convince us that just a few incidents are legendary or mythical, why may this not be true of all? May not Jesus be a lay-figure dressed up to suit the fancy of different sets of believers? It is but a step from this conception of Jesus as a peg on which men could hang their hopes and speculations to an attempt to interpret the rise of Christianity in terms of the schoolboy's recipe for making a pipe —take a hole and pour lead round it!

Think again of the many lives of Jesus that have been written during the last hundred years and that continue to pour from the press. Does the quest of the historic Jesus show any clear line of advance, any approximation to an agreed reading of his story? Schweitzer, in his brilliant survey of this quest, suggests, not indeed that Jesus did not exist, but that he remains a stranger and unknown. The picture drawn by liberal theologians, he claims, has been shown to be unhistorical. Guignebert who contributes the volume on Jesus to the great library on "The evolution of humanity," which is appearing in France under the editorship of Henri Berr, is very radical in his scepticism. He believes in a historic person behind the Christian movement, but he doubts whether we can be sure even that his name was Jesus! Modern interpreters present Jesus now as a sublime ethical teacher and now as an apocalyptic dreamer, at one time as a convinced pacifist and at another as a social revolutionary, a kind of super-Bolshevist. Where interpretations differ so violently, must not the controlling facts be few and uncertain, and does it not seem that writers pick and choose from the evidence of the gospels just those items which confirm their prejudices? Are there any facts to guide us? May it not be that men fashioned Christ to meet their varying needs and desires from the very first?

The main consideration, however, that favours the Christ-myth theory lies in the accumulation of parallels, actual or alleged, to the traditions concerning Jesus, both in broad outline and in small details. The story of his miraculous birth, it is claimed, may be paralleled from the traditions attached to Buddha, Krishna and Mithras. The story of his death and resurrection suggests a variant on the theme of the dying and rising God. Were there not many Pagan Christs — Attis or Adonis, Osiris or Mithras? When strikingly similar stories are related of these Pagan mythical figures, and when Jesus was regarded as Lord, as a cult-god like these "Lords many" of the Pagan world, why should we suppose Jesus to be any more historical than Adonis or Osiris? Then the teaching of Jesus turns out not to be so original as his devout followers have supposed. It can in many particulars at least be paralleled from Jewish and Gentile sources. As for the ministry of healing, Jesus may be as mythical a figure as the god, Asclepios. There is no teaching and no miracle attributed to Jesus which may not have been borrowed from contemporary sources by devotees anxious to glorify their cult-god. While we need not assume direct borrowing, it is plausible to argue that the existence of such parallels proves the possibility and probability of invention.

Confronted by considerations such as these, we must admit that the denial of the historicity of Jesus is not quite so irrational and fantastic as we probably at first supposed. There is a case to be weighed and accepted or rejected. It is, however, worth noting that among historians whose concern is to find out what really happened in the past, the Christ-myth does not meet with acceptance. Whatever the personal attitude of the trained student of history may be, he regards as undeniable fact the assertion that Jesus Christ suffered under Pontius Pilate, was crucified, dead and buried. As to other clauses of the Apostles'

Creed, the historian is bound to be more reticent. " Conceived of the Holy Ghost, born of the Virgin Mary . . . rose again the third day, ascended into heaven "—with regard to the events included in these affirmations, the historian may be profoundly sceptical. He will, however, make two assertions with great confidence. These clauses of the creed represent convictions concerning the nature and destiny of an actual person who really lived, and the belief that on the third day this historical character rose from the dead is much more primitive and much more fundamental to the movement known as Christianity than the beliefs regarding his birth and his ascension. Faith in the resurrection made the church.

Christ-myth theories appeal to those who imagine that the origins of Christianity are wrapt in profound mystery. It must be admitted that owing to the nature of our sources many questions about the beginnings of Christianity cannot be answered with any certainty. The critical and indeed hypercritical scrutiny to which the New Testament documents are being constantly subjected throws into relief every obscurity, every ambiguity, every discrepancy and every limitation in the evidence at our disposal. The inspection of so many dubious trees makes it difficult for us sometimes to discern the obvious wood. Yet the historian will not allow that there is any central mystery about the rise of Christianity. It began in Palestine in the reign of Tiberius when some Jews recognized a Galilean prophet, named Jesus, as the Messiah whose coming had been often foretold and long desired. The title

"Messiah" (in Greek, Christ) means "the Anointed One," and was the title given to the heaven-sent king who was to liberate Israel and judge and save mankind. The first Christians acclaimed Jesus as the coming king, in spite of the fact that he was put to death as a false Messiah and because they were convinced that he had been raised from the dead. A decisive factor in the development of Christianity as a world-religion was the discernment of a converted Pharisee, Saul of Tarsus, who realized that faith in a crucified Messiah meant the end of Judaism for every one who accepted it. All historians recognize that within a generation, Jesus was regarded as Christ and Lord, as the incarnation of the pre-existent Wisdom or Word of God. Through what stages and through what experiences and influences his followers came to entertain these beliefs, we do not know exactly. That they did entertain such beliefs regarding a historic person is beyond all reasonable doubt.

Before we examine the case for the Christ-myth, it may be worth while to observe that it does not appear to convince anyone unless he comes to the inquiry with certain presuppositions. Doubts regarding the historical existence of Jesus Christ are advanced only by persons who wish to establish preconceived ideas as to the nature of religion or as to the nature of history, and as we shall see, such doubts can only be maintained by distorting and misinterpreting the evidence and by flouting every recognized canon of literary and historical criticism.

Christ-myth theories find favour with rationalists who regard religion as illusion, and with mystical idealists who regard every entanglement of religion with historic fact as a degradation of a pure spiritual faith. Those who wish to destroy religion and those who wish to refine it unite in the endeavour to prove Jesus to be a fictitious creation. Moreover, those who resent the rôle of great men in history, and who wish to find the heroes of the human story in communities, classes or masses, are ready to believe that Jesus is at best a lay-figure and most probably the mythical embodiment of the aspirations and desires of some oppressed class, or of a frustrated generation of men. Students of religion, impressed with the influence of collective emotion, as well as sociologists of various schools, accept Christ-myth theories which exalt the group and deny the significance of the individual personality.

A brief survey of the literature of the Christ-myth will show how these differing tendencies are represented. The robust rationalist standpoint is best interpreted in the writings of the late J. M. Robertson, whose monumental works, *Christianity and Mythology* (1900), and *Pagan Christs* (1903), form a rich quarry on which others draw. Mr. Robertson was the friend and disciple of Charles Bradlaugh. He admired Bradlaugh's courage and honesty and wholeheartedly shared his convictions. He was familiar with the way in which Bradlaugh had been excommunicated and anathematized by narrow-minded orthodoxy, when as a Sunday School teacher he ventured to raise questions about the Bible. He had witnessed the disgraceful treatment meted out to Bradlaugh by political opponents in the name of religion. He was also aware of the abuse and obloquy which had been heaped on Bradlaugh and Mrs. Besant when they sought to spread knowledge on sex and birth-control in a way that offended Victorian standards. For J. M. Robertson, the Christian religion was identified with intellectual dishonesty. He saw in it nothing but a bar to scientific and moral progress. Belief in the supernatural in any shape or form was, in J. M. Robertson's judgment, an illusion, for he had embraced the two strange irrational dogmas of popular rationalism. He believed first that there is no intelligence in the universe higher and other than our own, and second that we, intelligent human beings, are the accidental outcome of natural forces devoid alike of intelligence and purpose. He did not at first question the historical existence of Jesus. He rejected out of hand all stories involving miracle, stories of visions of angels or of the driving out of demons, stories of miraculous healings or of apparent interferences with nature. For a time, he accepted Jesus as a historical character who lived and taught and died. But later he came to believe that the whole gospel-tradition was so steeped in supernaturalism that none of it is trustworthy. And if Jesus could be shown to be a myth, it would surely be a final demonstration of the illusory deceptive character of all religious faith. The denial of the historicity of Jesus would give the death-blow to a superstition that has per-suaded men to do and endure so much evil.

Robert Blatchford in *God and My Neighbour* (1903) and Philip Vivian, now Vivian Phelps,

in *The Churches and Modern Thought* (1906)
popularized the findings of J. M. Robertson. A
more scholarly defence and elaboration of his
theories has been undertaken by Mr. L. G.
Rylands, whose little book *Did Jesus Ever Live?*
(1935) is the most convenient recent statement
in short compass of the essential features of
the Christ-myth hypothesis. From the same
rationalist standpoint, Mr. Thomas Whittaker,
in *The Origins of Christianity* (1904), sought to
combine the findings of J. M. Robertson with the
critical positions of the Dutch professor, Van
Manen, regarding the Acts of the Apostles and
the letters attributed to St. Paul.

For fear lest any innocent reader of his book
should regard it as an attack upon the Christian
religion, Mr. Rylands in his foreword points out
that many other upholders of the Christ-myth
have undertaken the disproof of the historicity of
Jesus in the interest of religion. It is among
German authors that this tendency is best represented, and the tendency has often been associated
with Hegelianism. Indeed before Hegel, Lessing
had asserted that the eternal truths of reason
cannot be dependent on the contingent facts of
history, and religion, it is assumed, affirms spiritual
principles whose truth must exhibit a similar
independence. If we understand the nature of
spiritual religion and ethical ideals, then historical
happenings are at best of but secondary importance. We may then be indifferent to history, and
if we find popular devotion elevating what is
secondary to a position of primary importance, it
may be the duty of the spiritually enlightened to

knock away these historical props. If with Tolstoi we regard the Sermon on the Mount as containing the essence of Christianity, we may also with Tolstoi regard it as a matter of indifference whether the Sermon represents the actual teaching of a real person or not. The appeal of the story of the Good Samaritan remains unaltered, whether Jesus actually said it or whether it is merely put in his mouth. The kernel of Christianity for the Hegelian is not the historic incarnation, but the general truth of incarnation, the union of God and man, the truth that in God we live and move and have our being, the truth that human consciousness may represent or does represent the movement of Absolute Spirit. Since the story of Jesus suggests such truth to us and brings it into the stream of consciousness, that is all that matters. The extent to which the truth of incarnation was realized in a particular historic person is neither here nor there. From this standpoint, Strauss entered upon his radical criticism of the gospel-tradition. He certainly believed in a historic Jesus, but he was convinced that the gospels in the main depicted Jesus not as he was, but as his followers believed he must have been. J. M. Robertson suggested that Strauss occupied a gyratory position, unable to decide between two assumptions, one, that Jesus created the Church, and the other, that the Church created the figure of Jesus. It throws much light on Robertson's mentality that he regarded those assumptions as mutually exclusive. Strauss showed his continued hold on the realities of history, when he recognized that the Christian

Church cannot be explained at all without the existence and influence of a creative personality and when he assumed that the founder of a religious movement would be enshrined in an idealizing tradition.

Bruno Bauer, another Hegelian, went a good deal further than Strauss. In 1842, the Prussian government deprived him of his license to teach theology on account of his heterodox opinions, and his critical work betrays a natural animus against orthodoxy and orthodox theologians. The silencing of Bauer was one of the events which drove Karl Marx to the Left. Bauer believed that the historic figure of Jesus was a fictitious creation of the evangelist Mark. and he thought that Christianity was a morbid other-worldly religion that originated in the frustration, the failure of nerve, of Greco-Roman society in the time of the Cæsars.

The modern Christ-myth controversy was precipitated by the work of a philosopher, Arthur Drews, who wrote expressly in the interests of a religious pantheism. His book, *The Christ-myth,* was first published in 1910. The concluding section on the religious problem of the present day is most illuminating. Drews is a monist, that is to say, he believes that reality is all of a piece, consists of the same kind of stuff throughout. But he is not a materialist like Ernst Haeckel, the author of *The Riddle of the Universe.* For Drews, reality consists of a single all-inclusive process and God is immanent within it, and not in any sense outside and beyond it. To attach a special significance to an incarnation in Jesus is to obscure the truth that God is present in every man and in all nature and all history. The truth contained in the Christian doctrine of redemption may be defined as follows. The life of the world is God's life: the development of humanity, full of conflict and suffering, is the history of a divine struggle and passion: the process of the world is the process of a God who in each individual creature, strives, suffers, conquers and dies in order in the religious consciousness of man to overcome the limits of finiteness and anticipate his future triumphs over all the suffering of the world. The chief hindrance to the acceptance of this monistic religion and world-view is the belief in the historic actuality of a unique and unsurpassed personal Redeemer. So Drews set out to destroy this obstacle, not primarily because a straightforward survey of the evidence points to a denial of the historicity of Jesus, but because such a denial seemed essential to his religious philosophy and to his reading of the religious need of the age.

A Dutch Hegelian, Professor Bolland, had expounded a similar view in 1907, and in England the writings of the Rev. Gilbert T. Sadler represent an allied standpoint. Sadler thinks the true form of primitive Christianity was a spiritual Gnosticism, a doctrine of redemption rather than faith in a personal redeemer. The gospels are allegories, like the *Pilgrim's Progress* of John Bunyan. In America, Professor W. B. Smith in *Ecce Deus* and other works championed the Christ-myth in the interests of this conception of true religion.

Arthur Drews directed his attack against Christian theism, and against an ethical dualism which insists that you cannot simply identify God with nature or claim that in history, whatever is, is right. He was bent on undermining the Liberal-Protestant picture of Jesus as ethical teacher and religious genius. He was prepared to deny the connection of the modern valuation of personal liberty with the original Christian gospel. Fundamentally, religion is a social phenomenon, and Christianity must have been in origin the product of a community-life. A Socialist Lutheran pastor in Bremen, Albert Kalthoff, in revolt against bourgeois liberalism, argued that primitive Christianity must have been rooted in the religious fellowship, in the community. His book, *The Rise of Christianity* (Tr: by McCabe, 1901), traced Christianity back to communistic movements among the proletarians of the big cities in the Roman Empire. The veteran Social Democrat, Karl Kautsky, presented a similar view in his elaborate study of *The Foundations of Christianity* (1904). Kalthoff and Kautsky have said all that can be said, or at least all that is worth saying, in favour of the hypothesis that Christianity is essentially a group-movement independent of the influence of any outstanding personality.

After the war, a further contribution to the statement of the Christ-myth case was made from a fresh angle by a medical man in France. P. L. Couchoud reopened the whole controversy in a little book called *The Enigma of Jesus* (1924). He had been struck by the strength of the imagination in neurotic patients, and he argued that the figure of Jesus is a purely imaginary creation derived from

24

the visions of men like the proto-martyr Stephen and Paul the apostle to the Gentiles.

The exponents of the Christ-myth appear then to be guided and inspired by presuppositions of the kind which we have just outlined—presuppositions drawn from rationalism and philosophic idealism, from sociology and morbid psychology. Those who entertain the same presuppositions are naturally attracted to such interpretations of Christian origins. And there are other reasons why a wider public is drawn to the Christ-myth and perhaps is inclined to give it more favourable consideration than it really deserves. In the first place, scholars and thinkers of distinction, who would never definitely commit themselves to the thesis in its entirety, yet out of chivalry or out of sympathy with rationalism commend the writings of the Christ-myth school to the general public and suggest that though they should not be swallowed whole, there may be or there must be something in them. In this spirit, Sir James G. Frazer wrote a cautious non-committal preface to M. Couchoud's little book, *The Enigma of Jesus,* and Professor Gilbert Murray flattered the book with an extended favourable review. In more general terms, Bertrand Russell affects to regard the historical existence of Jesus as an open question, and the late G. Lowes Dickinson took up a similar position in his *Religion, a Criticism and a Forecast.* He suggested that those who had watched the process of idealization in other religions would be very distrustful of the picture of Jesus in the gospels, and he thought that those who knew the difficulties and doubts surrounding all historical inquiries would seek elsewhere than in history the basis of their belief and conduct.

In the second place, while a writer like Mr. Rylands may be free from anti-Christian bias, the Rationalist Press Association certainly is not. The literature of the Christ-myth is pushed and advertised by the R.P.A. in order to discredit Christianity. Under pressure it is said from the author, himself a member, the Association published F. C. Conybeare's vigorous criticism of J. M. Robertson's positions, in *The Historical Christ*. But the R.P.A. does not draw attention to Conybeare's book as they do, constantly, to the works of J. M. Robertson, or L. G. Rylands. They do not include F. C. Conybeare's book in the Thinkers' Library alongside of J. M. Robertson's *Short History of Christianity* and Vivian Phelips' *The Churches and Modern Thought*. Yet this is what they would do, if they were guided primarily by the love of truth and did not exist to secure an artificial circulation for anti-Christian propaganda.

In the third place, many people assume that the more bizarre and sensational a reading of the past is, the more likely it is to be true. Some like to trace a hidden hand in history, the Freemasons for choice, and in the case of Christianity, the Essenes or the Lamas of Thibet. Others suffer from the reading of detective fiction which fosters the belief that the obvious clues are all misleading, while the most petty and obscure detail will turn out to be most significant. People with this kind of mentality find the evidence for the Christ-myth most convincing and plume themselves on their acute perception of mysteries that elude ordinary common sense.

Lastly, there is deep-seated in many of us a real antagonism to Jesus and particularly to the position claimed for him as mediator between God and man. The whole idea of mediation is revolting to many minds. There still exists what John Foster called, " the aversion of men of cultivated taste to evangelical religion." Even to acknowledge a debt to Jesus as a creative power in history is repugnant to some men. Many are strengthened in their antagonism to Jesus, by the sentimental devotion that has gathered round his person and his cross. From sentimental hymns to devotions to the sacred wounds or the sacred heart, there is such a thing as a Jesus-olatry which offends both men of intellect and men of spiritual discernment. Would it not be a relief if we could relegate the figure of Jesus to the realm of myth? Moreover, the demands put into his lips are stern and inexorable. It would be easier to evade their challenge if we could dissociate them from the actualities of history. If Jesus were the figment of popular imagination, he would be more manageable and less baffling, less humiliating and more negligible. In this region, one may suspect, lie the deeper reasons why the Christ-myth hypothesis appears attractive and credible to not a few.

The task before us is now clear. We must examine by the standards of historical inquiry the case presented by those who deny the historicity of Jesus. We must ask first, how they account for the rise of Christianity when they have eliminated Jesus. In this connection we shall consider two propositions put forward as fundamental by J. M. Robertson, one of which—the assumption of a pre-

Christian cult of a Jesus-God—is essential to any form of the Christ-myth. I shall then endeavour to justify by illustrations my contention that the exponents of the Christ-myth do not and cannot deal fairly with the evidence at our disposal, and sin against the canons of literary and historical criticism. We may finally consider the questions: What is the religious significance of the historicity of Jesus? and what do we know about the historic Christ?

CHAPTER II

IS THE STORY OF THE CRUCIFIXION A MYTH?

THOSE who enter the world of Christ-myth speculation will appreciate the feelings of Aeneas when he
visited the lower world. The entrance to Hades
was beset by shadowy elusive figures, which Aeneas
could neither combat nor embrace. Nothing sub-
stantial or enduring met his grasp. So the inquirer
who seeks to know how Christianity arose without
a historic Jesus, is confronted with a crowd of
empty conjectures and constantly shifting assumptions.

He will be asked to believe that, unknown to
Josephus and Philo, there existed in Jewry in the
first century of our era, a number of sects of the
most varied character and diverse names. Ebionites,
Nazarenes, Naassenes, Ophites, Peratae, Elkesaites,
Mandaeans and what-not fill the stage. Christianity
began as a fusion of beliefs and practices, associated
with these sects. Some were practising human
sacrifice, or at least were so alive to the memories
of human sacrifice that they possessed and performed a ritual-drama based on actual human

sacrifice. Others were the initiates of a mystery-cult centred upon a Jesus-God who was a variant of the God who died and rose again. Others again pinned their faith to lofty teachings about the Wisdom and Word of God. Some believed in a suffering Messiah, others in a world-conquering Messiah. Some claimed to be true Jews and practised the Law: others rejected the Old Testament and its God. Somehow or other all these divergent views were amalgamated to make the Christian religion and the Catholic Church, and somehow or other curiously enough all the sects which contributed to the mixture subsequently got dissatisfied with it and left the new movement. It is very difficult to say, how or when or why or by whom the fusion was effected. Perhaps after the Jewish war and the fall of Jerusalem in A.D. 70, these obscure sects were regarded as unpatriotic and were no longer tolerated. Persecution drove these groups to unite. Perhaps a clever set of leaders saw in the downfall of Judaism an opportunity to build up a fresh organization which might levy tribute on Gentile converts. Judaism no longer appealed. A religious community whose faith embodied a fusion of the ideas of the Logos, the Messiah and the dying and rising God, in the name, not the person, of Jesus, might occupy the ground which Judaism was forced to vacate. It is very obscure, of course, since the leaders of the Catholic Church have suppressed all the evidence which would enable believers in the Christ-myth to prove their case. However, fortunately in the fourth century, one imprudent Church Father lifted the curtain, and obscure data furnished by Epiphanius concerning the Nazarenes and Ebionites and others enabled W. B. Smith and Arthur Drews to find out the truth about the first century and to ignore or contradict or explain away a hundred and one plain statements in the New Testament documents, though even on their own arbitrary assumptions such statements are at least three centuries earlier than Epiphanius.

To pursue and run to earth all the hares started by the ingenious advocates of the Christ-myth would be a labour for Hercules. If the patience and time of the readers are not to be exhausted, it is necessary to concentrate on one or two main issues. The story of the arrest, trial and death of Jesus may well serve as our test-case. If it can be shown that the crucifixion is a myth, let us allow that the case against a historic Christ has been proved. If the contentions of the Christ-myth theorists fail to convince at this point, perhaps further examination of their conjectures is superfluous.

The oldest and most original statement of the case for regarding the story of the Cross as a myth is to be found in *Pagan Christs*, Part II, Chapter I, entitled " The sacrificed Saviour-God." I propose to deal with it in some detail, since the case there stated by Mr. J. M. Robertson is accepted in its entirety by such writers as Mr. Thomas Whittaker and Mr. L. G. Rylands, and his belief in a pre-Christian Jesus-God is regarded as axiomatic by almost all writers belonging to this way of thinking. In dealing with Mr. J. M. Robertson, one is going to headquarters. If the original teacher fails us, the theorists who depend on him are not likely to succeed.

I am the more anxious to examine this main section of *Pagan Christs* because Mr. Robertson himself directed attention to it and challenged criticism on the two main theses set forth in it. It is a melancholy task to take to pieces his ingenious and elaborate structures when he is no longer here to defend them with his wonted pertinacity and skill. Yet he always desired that his errors of fact should be corrected, and I offer my critical analysis of his assertions and arguments as a tribute to the memory of a writer whose courage and independence I admired even while I deplored what seemed to me to be the waste of intellectual power involved in his writings on Christian origins.

His theory of the Crucifixion-myth is summarized in two main propositions which are stated thus: (1) " That the Gospel story of the Last Supper, the Agony, the Betrayal, the Crucifixion and the Resurrection is demonstrably not originally a narrative, but a mystery-drama which has been transcribed with a minimum of modification ": and (2) " That the mystery-drama was inferrably an evolution from a Palestinian rite of human sacrifice in which the annual victim was ' Jesus, the Son of the Father.' "[1] The second proposition involves three distinct inquiries. When once the dramatic character of the Passion-story is demonstrated, it is necessary to show that the details are derived from a ritual of human sacrifice. Next, it must be shown that the Jews were familiar with human sacrifice, or better still actually practising this barbaric rite at the time when Christianity arose. Finally, grounds must be produced for inferring that such a

[1] *Pagan Christs*, Preface to second edition, p. xi.

practice was associated with an ancient pre-Christian cult of a hero-god called Jesus or Joshua. The first proposition will be the subject of our next chapter.

CHAPTER III

WAS THE STORY OF THE CRUCIFIXION DERIVED FROM A MYSTERY-PLAY?

We begin our closer study of the myth of the crucifixion with the examination of the thesis that the concluding sections of the gospel-narrative are demonstrably a transcript of a mystery-drama.

The internal evidence in support of this contention is drawn primarily from two characteristics of the narrative, the extraordinary compression of events, and the utter absence of descriptive detail. The following extracts will perhaps suffice to illustrate Mr. Robertson's treatment of these points. " In a genuine historical tradition," he asked, " why should that impossible huddling of the action, that crowding of the betrayal and trial into one night, have been resorted to? It does not help the story as a narrative for reading: it makes it on the contrary so improbable that only the hebetude of reverence can prevent anyone from seeing its untruth. The solution is instant and decisive when we realize that what we are reading is the bare transcription of a mystery-play framed on the principle of ' unity of time.' Further evidence of the

absolutely unhistorical character of the narrative is
found in the fact that the whole judicial process
takes place in the middle of the night, a time when,
as Renan notes, an Eastern city is as if dead. The
point is that the invention is of a kind obviously
conditioned by a dramatic purpose. In the dead
of night the authorities proceed to hunt up 'false
witnesses' throughout Jerusalem, because the
witnesses must be produced in the trial scene as
closely as possible on that of the capture: and the
process goes on till two give the requisite testimony." Another minor detail of the same kind is
discovered when we read that " When morning was
come, the priests and elders *who thus have had no
rest*,[1] take counsel afresh to put Jesus to death, and
lead him away, bound, to Pilate." So much for the
unnatural compression of the incidents.

In the second place Mr. Robertson was much
perplexed by a narrative which avoids description
either of places or persons. The transitions are
made from place to place, e.g. from the upper room
to Gethsemane, without any of the descriptive
touches characteristic of ordinary narrative. The
writer is clearly repeating the contents of a series
of dramatic tableaux. He has no interest in and
no material for, supplying any account of the
intervening events. All is dialogue or simple
action. The following are some of the most pertin-
ent passages in which Mr. Robertson developed this
argument:

"As the story stands, Jesus partakes with his
disciples of the Passover, an evening meal: and
after a very brief dialogue, they sing a hymn and

[1] Italics mine.—H.G.W.

proceed in the darkness to the mount of Olivet. *Not a word is said of what happened or was said on the way:*[1] the scene is simply changed to the mount: and there begin a new dialogue and action. A slight change of scene—*again effected with no hint of any talk on the way*[1]—is made to Gethsemane: and here the scanty details as to the separation from ' his disciples,' and the going apart with the three, indicate with a brevity obviously dramatic, the arrangement by which Judas—who was thus far with the party—would on the stage be enabled to withdraw. Had the story been first composed for writing, such an episode would necessarily have been described: *and something would naturally have been said of the talk on the way from the supper-chamber to the mount.*[1] What we are reading is the bare transcript of a primitive play, in which the writer has not here attempted to insert more than has been shown on the scene."

Similarly when the arrest is described, Judas reappears, " without the slightest account of what he has been doing in the interlude." The disciples forsake Jesus and flee: " and not a word is said of what they did in the interim: though any account of the episode, in the terms of the tradition concerning them, must have come through them."

Again, after the sentence of condemnation, we have the scene of Peter's denial. " Of what happens to the doomed God-Man in the interval there is not a hint: though it is just here that a non-dramatic narrative would naturally follow him most closely." Once more, throughout the narrative, " not a word is said of the *aspect* of Jesus, a

[1] Italics mine.—H.G.W.

point on which an original narrator, if writing to be read, or telling of what he had seen, would almost certainly have said something. In a drama, of course, no such details were needed: the suffering God-man was there on the stage, seen by all the spectators."

One other detail, to which Mr. Robertson drew attention, should be noted. In Matt. xxvi. 45 and 46, " in two successive sentences with no pause between, Jesus tells the sleeping three to sleep on and to arise. What has happened is either a slight disarrangement of the dialogue or the omission of an exit and an entrance." Mr. Robertson proposed an alteration in the order of verses 44 to 46, by which " the incongruity would be removed." He added " only in transcription from a dramatic text could it (the incongruity) have arisen " (p. 198).

So impressed was Mr. Robertson by this and kindred evidence that he described the finality of his demonstration in the following terms: " The theory of the dramatic origin of the coherent yet impossible story of the Supper, Agony, Betrayal, the two Trials and the Crucifixion is borne out *at every point by every detail*[1] of the structure of the story as we have it in transcription: and when this is once recognized, our conception of the manner of the origin of the gospels is at this point at least placed on a new, we might say a scientific, basis " (p. 204).

We may start our scrutiny of this interesting essay in literary criticism by considering the last point first. The final speech of Jesus to the sleeping disciples is strange and contains an apparent

[1] Italics mine.—H.G.W.

contradiction. Possibly the first clause is to be
taken ironically, as Dr. Moffatt takes it in his trans-
lation. " Still asleep? Still resting? No more of
that! The hour has come, here is the Son of Man
betrayed into the hands of sinners. Come, get up,
here is my betrayer close at hand." Possibly there
is a rapid change of emotion. Jesus, making a concession to the disciples' weakness, " Sleep on now
and take your rest," suddenly breaks off as he hears
Judas approaching. But if there is some disorder
in the text, such as Mr. Robertson supposed, the
incongruity might arise just as readily in copying
out a historical narrative as in transcribing a
dramatic text. If Mr. Robertson's main contentions were sound, his view of Matthew xxvi. 44-6,
might derive support from them, but in itself it
adds no weight to his demonstration.

What, then, are we to say of the broader arguments on which Mr. Robertson relied? Take first
the huddling together of events which is supposed
to be impossible history. Is it really incredible that
the arrest, trial and execution of Jesus should have
taken place within twenty-four hours or less? If the
trial and execution of Jesus happened at all, they are
more likely than not to have happened in a hurry.
It is natural to expect that the actual history would
lie open precisely to the kind of suspicion with
which Mr. Robertson viewed it. The hurried
removal of inconvenient individuals has occurred
over and over again in history, especially in the
East. Somewhat parallel instances of similar haste
may be found in the account of the death of
Stephen in Acts, in the story of the martyrdom of
Polycarp who was arrested overnight and burnt

next day after being examined and condemned by a proconsul, and in the reference to the proceedings of the high priest Ananus who had James the brother of the Lord put to death by stoning. (Josephus, Ant. xx, Ch. 9, §1.) All these stories may be fictions, but they cannot all be of dramatic origin, though they present the same huddling of events which in the gospels is to be attributed to dramatic purpose and the wish to preserve dramatic unity of time. The rapid succession of the closing scenes of the gospel—sufficiently explained in the gospels themselves by the desire of the rulers to get rid of Jesus before the feast—does not of itself require or even suggest the theory of dramatic origin.

The case for the mystery-drama depends not merely on the rapidity with which events transpire, but on the improbability of some of the particular events recorded. To Mr. Robertson it seemed incredible that the proceedings should have taken place at night, when as Renan says an Eastern city is as if dead. In spite of Renan, things do happen at night, even in Eastern cities. Sceptical readers who discount the gospels as historical narratives should not ignore their evidence as to social life. A bridegroom and his bride might return home at midnight and find the virgin watchers unprepared. Thieves did not always respect Renan's dictum. They broke into houses at night and the good man of the house would have kept awake if only he had known when to expect them. It is not beyond the bounds of possibility that high priests and members of the Sanhedrin should forgo a night's rest to get rid of Jesus. Indeed it is precisely because at night an Eastern city is as if dead, that the arrest of Jesus by night is historically probable. Renan's dictum strengthens the case for history and weakens the case for drama.

There is, however, one respect in which it seemed to Mr. Robertson that the story was flatly impossible. The authorities could not have spent a restless night hunting up witnesses in the dark, while Jerusalem slept. I should have thought it would have been very difficult if not impossible to represent such a hunt after witnesses on the stage. It is certainly possible history: as drama it is next to impossible. But let us grant that this midnight hunt after witnesses might by some pretty device have been included in the mystery-drama and let us concede that it is unlikely history. The point is unimportant since the incident is not in the text. Neither in Mark xiv. 55 nor in Matthew xxvi. 59 is there any reference to a search after witnesses. Moffatt translates correctly, " Now the high priests and the whole of the Sanhedrin tried to secure evidence against Jesus." The authorities did not proceed to hunt up witnesses. They were trying to get evidence from witnesses already present.

Like some other writers, Mr. Robertson misunderstood the expression in the authorized version, " the council sought witness against Jesus." He read " witness " as if it meant " witnesses." The Greek is quite clear. It has the abstract word for " evidence." When I pointed this out to Mr. Robertson, he replied to me in a letter, " As to the ' seeking for evidence,' I remain at a loss to understand how you can find any *plausibility* in your idea that it meant examining witnesses already collected. If that were meant to be said, the statement would have been that ' they brought forth witnesses.' It is the ' ezētoun ' (the Greek verb, ' they sought ') that is the crux. Your original idea of ' sifting ' will never do : if the evidence had been previously collected, it would have been sifted before the trial. Would any prosecutor in a real trial bring up his witnesses without knowing what they were likely to say? "[1] The verb " they sought " is indeed the crux. It is used technically of judicial inquiry. The corresponding noun is found in Acts xxv. 20, where Festus explains to King Agrippa that he felt at a loss *about the method of inquiry*[2] into the topics involved in Paul's case. My idea is not just a plausible suggestion. If it is not the only possible, it is certainly the most natural meaning of the Greek expression used.

The point is of some interest because the correct understanding of the phrase explains the real nature of the so-called trial before the high priest and the Sanhedrin. Again and again we are told that this cannot be a historical trial because it is utterly illegal and contravenes the normal rules of procedure in the Sanhedrin. Incidentally it is curious how concerned some critics are about illegality. Thus, we are asked to doubt the martyrdom of Stephen because the Jews had not the legal right to inflict capital punishment. Apparently rationalists who regard contraventions of natural law as necessarily unhistorical, imagine that man's law must be similarly inviolable. Illegalities, like

---

[1] Unpublished letter of Oct. 13, 1917.
[2] Moffatt's rendering.

miracles, do not happen. Alas! historic facts refuse
to confirm this simple faith! Had it been as full
of illegalities as many critics suppose, the trial
before the Sanhedrin might still be history. But
actually this so-called trial was a preliminary
examination of prisoner and witnesses before
presenting the case to the Roman governor. The
phrase " seeking for evidence " so far from intro-
ducing an absurdity like a midnight hunt for witnesses into the story, reveals the true character of
the historic happening recorded.[1]

Though Mr. Robertson stressed this particular
incident, which arises as we have seen from a misunderstanding of a single phrase, as the most important detail suggestive of drama rather than
of history, he and his followers find difficulty in
other features of the narrative. He urged that at
least the prayer of Jesus in Gethsemane must be
dramatic invention since the disciples are represented as being at a distance and asleep and so
could not have heard it. At first sight there seems
to be some force in this argument, but it will not
stand examination. Professor T. W. Manson's comment in his book *The Teaching of Jesus* (p. 104,
n. 1) is fully justified.

The arguments by which it is sought to prove that
the words of the prayer are not authentic are extremely
unconvincing. They hinge on two main points: the
distance of Jesus from the chosen three, and the fact
that they fell asleep. To make the former at all effective the " little further on " of Mark xiv. 35 has to be
stretched beyond what is reasonable. The latter has

---

[1] Mr. Robertson remained unconvinced on this point. See
his answer to my criticisms in *The Jesus-Problem*, pp. 99-102.

no force unless we make the supposition, whose absurdity is evident as soon as it is made, that all three companions of Jesus composed themselves to slumber as soon as he took the first step away from them, and were sound asleep when he began to pray. . . . The text of Mark leaves us perfectly free to believe that Jesus remained within hearing of his three companions: that he prayed aloud, at the beginning of his prayer, if not throughout: and that one or other of the disciples heard what was said before sleep overtook them.

But there is another possibility which deserves consideration. One little incident peculiar to Mark's narrative relates that when all the disciples forsook Jesus and fled, " one young man did follow him, with only a linen sheet thrown round his body, but when the young men seized him he fled away naked, leaving the sheet behind him." (Mark xiv. 51, 52.) It has often been suggested that the young man was the evangelist himself and this trivial incident may be the artist's signature in the corner of his picture. The story of Gethsemane may then rest on the evidence of Mark, and in any case, the young man may be Mark's informant. The detail adduced as proof of dramatic invention is probably the reminiscence of an actual eye-witness.

Before we take up Mr. Robertson's second broad argument in support of his thesis, namely, the absence of descriptive detail, it may be well to touch on two other points which are supposed to throw doubt on the narrative of the trial of Jesus. One is the part played by the crowd and the other the conduct of Pilate. " It is very hard to understand how the crowd who acclaimed Jesus (on the occasion of the triumphal entry) as 'Son of David,' could, a few days later, have clamoured for his execution."[1] Personally, I do not feel the difficulty. The fickleness of crowds is a well-known phemonenon. But the difficulty is non-existent. The supposition that the crowd which welcomed Jesus on his entry into Jerusalem was the same as the crowd which cried out, " Crucify him," is purely gratuitous. The gospels nowhere suggest the identification. It is just a fancy of commentators. With a million or more pilgrims in Jerusalem for the feast, there would be more than enough material for two distinct crowds!

As to Pilate, we know from Josephus that he was hard and overbearing and that he could be brutal and ruthless. In the gospel-narratives, it is said, he appears weak and vacillating. The Pilate of history, if he had believed in the innocence of Jesus, would have defied the Jewish rulers and released him. Perhaps—yet I doubt whether there is any fundamental psychological inconsistency in the character of Pilate as drawn by Josephus and as presented in the gospels. A vein of self-distrust, of weakness and vacillation may well have underlain Pilate's harshness and brutality, and the circumstances of the trial of Jesus may naturally have brought it to the fore. If, as seems likely, Pilate had been privy to the arrest of Jesus and had agreed with the chief priest that he should be put out of the way for fear of an uproar among the people, then he may have hesitated when Jesus appeared

---

[1] L. G. Rylands, *Did Jesus Ever Live?*, p. 46. Cf. Robertson, *Jesus and Judas*, p. 48.

before him and when he realized how thin the case against Jesus really was. Yet his hesitation would not carry him so far as to defy the rulers of Israel. After all, there is always trouble at the passover. Caiaphas may be right. It is expedient that one man die for the people. And Jesus has confessed to the charge, and does nothing to help Pilate in the latter's efforts to release him. Pilate might naturally say to himself, I have done my best for him and I can do no more. I see no improbability in this as history, but if the evangelists have mis-represented Pilate's character and conduct (and they may have done so, since they tend to minimize Pilate's responsibility, and to maximize the responsibility of Jewish rulers and people), it is difficult to see how Mr. Robertson's hypothesis helps to explain the misrepresentation. No dramatic necessity underlies the evangelists' por-trayal of Pilate.

What then are we to make of the other features of the narrative which in Mr. Robertson's judgment demonstrate its dramatic origin? He points to omissions which he would not expect in historical narrative. He thinks a genuine history would not have omitted details of conversation during journeys,[1] would have indulged in personal descrip-tions and would have explained what various characters were doing in various intervals. Un-doubtedly the story is, as he claims, intensely

---

[1] It is probable that Mark xiv. 27-31 with its parallel in Matthew xxvi. 30-5, is to be understood as a conversation on the way to the Mount of Olives. The previous verse may legitimately be translated, " And having sung a hymn they went out towards the Mount of Olives." Mr. Robertson over-stated his case.

dramatic. But then the whole of Mark's gospel bears the same character. Rapid transitions effected in a sentence with no account of what happens during the process: absence of anything in the way of description, except speech and action: no reference to the *aspect* of the central figures: — these are features of Mark's gospel as a whole, not of the last two or three chapters in particular. These dramatic qualities belong not only to Mark, but to all the gospels and to all popular story-telling, especially in the East. The incidents narrated in the gospels took shape in oral tradition, and so would reflect the characteristics of popular story-telling. An Irishman might justly claim that all Biblical stories are full of rapid transitions, omitted conversations and interims unaccounted for. Unlike modern novelists, an ancient raconteur rarely described personal appearance or personal emotion.

A very good instance of the fallacy we are now considering may be drawn from the Shakespeare-Bacon controversy. One main argument of the Baconians seems to be that Shakespeare's constant use of legal terms proves him to have been a lawyer and therefore Bacon. Mr. Robertson, in his masterly exposure of the Baconian heresy, showed that every Elizabethan dramatist is full of legal tags. All the expressions supposed to be peculiar to Shakespeare are extant in Greene or Ben Jonson or some other writer. In other words, the mistake of the Baconians consists in providing a special theory to explain a peculiarity in Shakespeare which does not exist. In the same way Mr. Robertson advanced a special theory to account for the dramatic features of the closing chapters of Mark or of Matthew, which features those chapters share with the rest of the gospel and indeed with all popular story-telling, at least in the Ancient Semitic world. Thus Mr. Robertson ardently embraced as a demonstration in *Pagan Christs* the very fallacy he had exposed so decisively in the case of the Baconians.

It is hardly necessary to pursue this side of the subject much further, but in view of Mr. Robertson's belief that his theory is borne out at every point by every detail of the structure of the story, it is worth while to mention that he found great difficulty with some details, and that he accounted for others by reading too much into them. Thus we learn that, after the evidence is given, " Jesus is questioned, condemned, buffeted and (presumably) led away: and Peter, remaining on the scene, denies his Lord, and is convicted of treason by the crowing of the cock." The word " presumably " is judicious, as the presumption received no support from the text. The natural interpretation of the text is that the evangelist is describing two simultaneous incidents, not two successive scenes in a drama. Luke certainly assumes that this is what Mark intends, for in Luke xxii. 61, Jesus (still on the scene) turns and looks on Peter. But the natural interpretation would not suit Mr. Robertson's case, so an element of presumption had to come in in order to make every detail support the dramatic theory.

It would be tedious to dwell on other difficulties in the way of this theory of a gospel mystery-play, though we may note two or three points. First there is no clear evidence of a religious use of drama among the Jews parallel to Greek mystery-dramas. Mr. Robertson therefore was obliged to assume this without proof. The Jews were notoriously deficient in the dramatic art, and it is in the highest degree unlikely that any mystery-drama existed among them in the first century. Secondly Mr. Robertson's theory that this mystery-play was " the very womb and genesis of the whole Christian faith," involves the belief that " the cult developed rather in the larger than in the smaller Hellenistic cities and it would need a fairly strong group to produce such a mystery-play." (*Pagan Christs*, p. 204.) So far as the Synoptic gospels are concerned, this belief seems to be contrary to fact, since the background is genuinely Palestinian, and decidedly Jewish, not Hellenistic.[1] Thirdly, the drama of Mr. Robertson's imagination must be classed either with Greek mystery-acts or with later mediæval religious plays. But so far as we are aware, neither in the one nor the other did the Aristotelian principles of tragedy hold good. There was no attempt in either to preserve the unity of time. If such a mystery-play ever existed, we have no reason to suppose that events would be compressed out of deference to Aristotle. This cannot be the explanation of the characteristic of the assumed gospel-drama on which Mr. Robertson laid most stress. The compression was due to the nature of the subject-matter. If there was a drama, it is more likely that this huddling of events is derived from the history on which it was based,

[1] Mr. Robertson's attempt to circumvent this difficulty will be found in *The Jesus-Problem*, p. 74.

than that it was imposed by a poetic principle of which the average Christian had never heard and for which no religious dramatist or devotee cared in the least.[1] But it is an endless task to discuss which is the more probable explanation of the most salient feature of a drama in whose existence one has no reason whatever to believe.

[1] Mr. Robertson, in a note on page 198 of *Pagan Christs*, admitted that the drama he was seeking must have been non-literary, but held that it would be classical in regard to the unities. There is no evidence for this positive assertion, which is deduced from the necessity of his own hypothesis.

CHAPTER IV

THE MYSTERY-PLAY AND SOURCE-CRITICISM: CAN THE STORY OF THE CRUCIFIXION BE TRACED BACK TO A DISTINCT AND INDEPENDENT SOURCE?

BEFORE going further, we must say something of the critical position presupposed in Mr. Robertson's investigations. Not only did he erroneously regard certain dramatic qualities as peculiar to the closing chapters of Matthew or Mark, but he also assumed that there was no connection between the narrative of the arrest, trial, and execution of Jesus and the traditions regarding his public ministry in the earlier sections of the gospels. All the material he wished to include in his mystery-drama was to be kept distinct and separate from all that is told of Jesus as teacher and healer, and in making this separation he claimed to have the support of modern critical opinion. He wrote, "The higher criticism has recognized that the story of the betrayal and the rest do not belong to the earlier matter of Gospels. The analysis of the school of Bernhard Weiss, as presented by Mr. A. J. Jolley, makes the 'Primitive Gospel' end with the scene of the anointing. I hold that scene to have been also dramatic, and to have been first framed as a prologue to the Mystery-play: but the essential point is that all that portion which I have above treated as a Mystery-play is an addition to a previously existing document." (*Pagan Christs*, p. 201.) This position Mr. Robertson maintained to the last. In his final most vigorous restatement of his theory in a little book, *Jesus and Judas*, he claimed to have " textual evidence which goes to prove that the five-act story of the Supper, the Agony, the Capture, the Crucifixion and the Resurrection, as it stands in the first two of the synoptics, was a *dramatic* text, reduced to narrative form with a minimum of necessary narrative, and added to the gospels after these or some of them were in circulation." (*Jesus and Judas*, p. 70.) Actually, there is no textual evidence which goes to prove this thesis, and there is no school of higher criticism which recognizes that the story of the betrayal and the rest do not belong to the earlier matter of the gospels or that the story of the Supper, the Agony, the Capture, the Crucifixion and the Resurrection has been added to the gospels after these or some of them were in circulation. Bernhard Weiss may have believed in a " Primitive Gospel " which did not contain a passion-narrative, just as most scholars to-day believe in a source common to Matthew and Luke, which was primarily a record of the teaching of Jesus and did not include an account of Passion-week. But Weiss certainly did not believe in the story of the Cross as a late addition to Mark's gospel. He did not believe that the five-act story which Mr. Robertson arbitrarily isolated ever existed as a separate document. Bernhard Weiss derived much of Mark from the Primitive Gospel as he conceived it, but the story of the Cross is not the only material which he assigned to another source. Weiss coupled chapter xi. and the bulk of chapter xii. with chapters xiv. and xv., as belonging to the same source.[1] Incidentally, the first two verses of Mark, chapter xiv., must be narrative and cannot be drama: also they cannot on literary grounds be separated from the remainder of the chapter. The essential point is that the school of Bernhard Weiss did not provide Mr. Robertson with his indispensable foundation, and he was not justified in assuming it without further proof. His theory of the dramatic origin of the passion-narrative is an improbable solution of a non-existent literary problem.

If he had been acquainted with them, Mr. Robertson might have found more comfort in post-war developments in the critical study of the gospels. The Form-critics believe that the materials on which the gospels are based consisted in the main of detached stories, which fall into half a dozen classes. They also believe that the passion-narrative was told and retold as a distinct and separate story. This view would seem to justify Mr. Robertson or anyone else in putting forward a special theory of the origin of this particular narrative. On the other hand, no modern critic believes, and I am not sure that any critic has ever believed the naïve theory that Mark xiv. and xv. was added as an afterthought

[1] See *Synoptic Problem for English Readers*, p. 113.

to Mark i.-xiii. No modern critic believes that the passion-narrative does not belong to the earlier stratum of the traditions concerning Jesus. No modern critic believes that the passion-narrative derives from one sect, labelled Jesuine, and the Sermon on the Mount from another labelled Christist, and the miracles of healing from a third labelled anything you like. There never was a " Primitive Gospel " with no story of the passion. There never was a story of the passion which did not imply a knowledge of the events of the public ministry of Jesus both in Galilee and Jerusalem. A theory which assumes that the story of the Cross comes from a group which knew only the mystery-cult of a dying and rising God and which was unaware of a divine teacher, finds no support at all in textual evidence and literary analysis. In any case, Mr. Robertson's appeal to higher criticism was ill-advised. He claimed support for the view that the passion-story was not part of the earlier material of the gospels, that it had a distinct origin and was a late addition to the Primitive Gospel. But he had also committed himself to the view that the mystery-drama was the womb and genesis of the whole Christian movement. As he wished to substantiate this view, his appeal to Bernhard Weiss was suicidal. The womb of the faith can hardly have been added as an appendix to the Primitive Gospel! In *Pagan Christs* (p. 201) he tried to safeguard himself, by adding, " Not that the play (in some form) was not older than the document, but that its transcription is later." He was not entitled to adopt this way of safeguarding his own position unless he was prepared to recognize that the same defence was valid against his attempt to discredit the story of the Cross as history. "Here even more than elsewhere the documents are invalid, seeing that in the Primitive Gospel as reconstructed by conservative criticism, the story of the trial and execution has confessedly no place. Whatever may have been the primary facts, the Gospel-story, framed long after the alleged event, and after a Jesus-memoir was already current, has no evidential value."[1] Even if these erroneous assertions were true, the critic who accepted them would have just as much right as Mr. Robertson to say, "Not that the Gospel-story of the Cross, in some form, was not older than the Jesus-memoir. It was written down and added to the memoir at a comparatively late date, but in its original form it was framed soon after the actual event and has undeniable evidential value!" In any case, Mr. Robertson's description of the higher criticism was mistaken and misleading.

[1] *Christianity and Mythology* (1st ed.), p. 394.

CHAPTER V

IT seems at first sight as if the break-down of the
demonstrable dramatic theory would take the
heart out of the discussion of the inferrable
sacrificial development on which the drama is
supposedly based. But in truth the second main
thesis continues to be of interest after the first
has been surrendered. If the story of the Cross
is not dramatic in character, it may still be
sacrificial in origin. The events, real or supposed, that form the subject-matter of the
narrative, may reflect an elaborate ritual of
human sacrifice. We have not disproved the
possible existence of such a ritual among the
post-exilic Jews, and a non-dramatic narrative
may be associated with a pre-Christian Jesus-cult.
  We turn then to consider the claim that
" Anthropological research leads us to trace the
gospel-story of the Crucifixion back to a ritual of
many variants in the East." It is assumed that
the gospel-drama took the place of an actual
sacrifice, and Mr. Robertson was glad to be able
to point to a probable instance of such a substitution of drama for rite, in the history of

human sacrifice in Rhodes. "The Rhodian rite points to the decisive development which we have yet to trace in the case of the gospel-story. For Porphyry incidentally mentions that the Rhodian sacrifice, after having subsisted long, had latterly been modified. As to the precise nature of the modification we have no further knowledge: but we are entitled to conclude that it was either a simple rite of mock-sacrifice or a mystery-drama. Both stages, indeed, would be natural, the step to the latter being dependent on the connection of the rite with a eucharist. But the essential point is that in this case . . . we have exactly the kind of transition from actual human sacrifice to a conventional rite of mock-sacrifice which our theory implies."[1] There is no reason why the history of Rhodes should not have repeated itself in Palestine. Nor need it be supposed that the Jews copied the Rhodian rite. It is enough that, like the Rhodians, they turned a rite of human sacrifice into a drama, the drama being " at bottom a perpetuation of the latest form of the primitive rite as it had been publicly performed."

The case of Rhodes is interesting, and we may have to return to it later, but the strength of Mr. Robertson's theory of sacrificial drama does not rest on what may seem a hasty generalization from a rather doubtful individual instance. Even if there is no record of any modification or trans-formation of human sacrifice into drama, the internal evidence from certain features of the gospel-story would still suffice to confer some

[1] *Pagan Christs*, p. 187.

probability on the sacrificial theory. We shall attempt to summarize his views on this head, and in the attempt the dangerous haziness surrounding them will become apparent. The critical examination of these theories must be deferred to later chapters, but the mere exposition of them will show the reader how unfortunate it is that Mr. Robertson, holding, as we have seen he did, that the drama was a perpetuation of a primitive sacrificial rite, forgot to tell us, what exactly was the earliest form of the drama, and what exactly was the latest form of the primitive rite.

Mr. Robertson's line of proof consists in showing that several particulars in the narrative of the Cross correspond or coincide with details of human sacrifice among savages the world over. He claimed that most of the features of the gospel-stories can be explained as definite sacrificial practices, and that some peculiar features are strange and out of place in a judicial execution, though they become intelligible as soon as we take into account their sacrificial source. It may be said at once that these latter details do give some colour to Mr. Robertson's argument. They form the most serious of the considerations which he advanced. And it was worth Mr. Robertson's while to draw attention to them, even though the theory he sought to base on them, is not thereby established.

To come then to some of the details: we may note that Mr. Robertson would see in the crucifixion of two thieves along with Jesus, a ritual practice parallel to that which obtained at Bundair in Jeypore, where "there were sacrificed to the

Sun-god at one festival *three*[1] victims, ' one at the east, one at the west, and the third in the centre of the village.' " As the presence of the two thieves is mentioned in the four gospels, we may assume that three victims suffered in the latest form of the primitive rite as it was publicly performed.

This feature of the crucifixion is not one which in itself rouses doubts as to the credibility of the event. It is rather a detail which Mr. Robertson was glad to bring within his theory, by means of a sacrificial parallel.

The next detail which we have to consider belongs to another category. It is surely perplexing that myrrhed wine, or wine mingled with gall, should be offered to Jesus on the way to the Cross. The drink is obviously a narcotic, and as obviously, narcotics have no place in an execution. The Romans would not alleviate the suffering in a punishment which was meant to be exemplary. Any such drink would be out of place in a narrative of a simple execution. But it is natural and frequent in connection with sacrifices. There are many instances among the Khonds and others of sacrificial victims being drugged to make them appear willing. The practice clearly hints at some such sacrificial ritual. Mr. Robertson further suggested that the use of gall in the rites of Demeter might account for the reference to gall in one of the gospels, and this theory would ascribe the draught to a religious usage.

It is worth noting that " there is no suggestion that any drink was offered to the two thieves: here we are dealing with a sacrificial ritual in

[1] Italics, Mr. Robertson's *Pagan Christs*, p. 115.

which only the central victim is a true sacrifice."[1]

The sacrificial explanation of the proffer of myrrhed wine thus compels a modification of the conception of the latest form of the primitive rite which was suggested by the parallel from Bundair. Having concluded that there must have been three victims, we now have to recognize that there was only one true victim on the last public occasion of the sacrifice. In other words, the discovery of the sacrificial character of the wine unfortunately destroys the worth of the parallel from Bundair, by denying a sacrificial character to two of the victims. Perhaps Mr. Robertson would have regarded them as quasi-victims, for, like many other theorists, he perceived the utility of that pleasing prefix. It throws such a comfortable cloak of respectability around conceptions whose emptiness forbids closer inspection.

Two incidents in St. John's gospel seem, like the narcotic, to be out of place in an execution, and to be susceptible of explanation from the side of human sacrifice. In that gospel we read that the legs of the thieves were broken and the side of Jesus pierced with a spear.

The silence of the Synoptics is supposed to show both details to be unhistorical, and the alleged purpose of the breaking of the legs is absurd. It would not fulfil the purpose suggested, that of hastening the death of the sufferers: it would only increase their agony. The spear-thrust seems equally unnecessary.[2]

[1] *Pagan Christs*, p. 120 n.
[2] Cf. *Pagan Christs*, p. 121.

All is clear, however, according to Mr. Robertson, if it is once realized that we are reading a story based on a sacrificial ritual. Among the Khonds, to ensure the appearance of willingness in the victim, the legs used to be broken to prevent unseemly struggles. This detail again is sacrificial, and in the latest form of the primitive rite, the two others who, as we have seen, were not victims in the full sense, must have been quasi-victims, since in respect of the breaking of their legs they are treated as victims. Probably the willingness of the chief victim in the latest performance of the rite was ensured by the narcotic, which, according to the evangelists, he would not drink, and the willingness of the minor victims was simulated by the breaking of their legs. The detail of the spear-thrust is similarly sacrificial. Strabo tells us that among the Albanians, when the festival day of the moon-goddess came, one of the sacred slaves " was *anointed* with a fragrant ointment and slain by being *pierced to the heart with a sacred lance through the side.* . . . Here we have a sacrifice corresponding in one notable detail to one of the gospel narratives, and having other marked features in common with other well-known rites of human sacrifice."[1] This particular detail does not appear to be associated with crucifixion in any sacrificial rite outside the gospels, but in the last public performance of the primitive rite, they must have been almost over-anxious that the victim should be perfectly willing, and when the effect of the narcotic wore off, or if, as the gospels suggest, the narcotic was

[1] *Pagan Christs*, p. 125.

refused, this more expeditious method was doubt-less adopted to ensure no mishap on so momentous an occasion.

It will be seen at once that the sacrificial inter-pretation of these details still further complicates the question, what was the latest form of the primi-tive rite, of which the drama was in the main a perpetuation?   Mr. Robertson attempts to deal with the difficulty by assuming that " the different narratives testify to the existence of a *ritual or rituals* of crucifixion or quasi-crucifixion, in vari-ants of which there had figured the two procedures of breaking the legs of the victim and giving him a narcotic."[1]   In the same way, " the detail of the spear-thrust in the side bestowed only on the ostensibly divine victim, suggests that in some similar ritual that may have been the mode of cere-monial slaying."[1]

Mr. Robertson's position then is something like this.   Main details, such as the number of the victims and the narcotic, come from the latest form of the primitive rite.   Details like the leg-breaking come from a variant in which this procedure figured.   The spear-thrust is derived from a ritual of quasi-crucifixion or perhaps from a sacrificial ritual which had no crucifixion, but which Mr. Robertson described by the convenient term ' quasi-crucifixion ' in order to hide the fact that he was combining entirely dissimilar rituals.

We can now consider other details.   The paying of a price to Judas by the priests doubtless comes from a sacrificial system in which the victim had to be purchased.   Mr. Robertson discovered a still

[1] *Pagan Christs*, p. 121.

earlier sacrificial custom enshrined in the gospels, and not merely in the story of the crucifixion. Readers of Prescott's *Mexico* or Rider Haggard's *Montezuma's Daughter* will remember that the sacrificial victims were treated royally and allowed great licence for a year before the sacrifice. In the most primitive practice of all, willing victims were apparently secured by the bribe of a year's riotous living. Mr. Robertson suggested that " the common belief of the early Church that the ministry of Jesus lasted for only one year may have (its) basis in the old usage," while " in the character of the Messiah as one who associated with publicans and sinners, in his association with women," and especially with the Magdalene, we may trace a similar survival of this most primitive sacrificial custom.[1]

Scientific worth is claimed for this theory on the ground that it colligates a number of isolated details in a surprising and satisfying manner. The very essence of science is to give meaning to a group of particulars by discovering within them a common principle. And Mr. Robertson certainly linked together in a wonderful way features of the gospel-narrative which no one had previously thought of connecting. He found his clue in the principle well known to anthropologists that the crucified Saviour-God, and indeed any victim destined for sacrifice, must appear to suffer willingly.

The Christian father Tertullian is aware of this, for he says: " Even the sacrificial victims are required to be of a willing mind."[2] This rule is

[1] *Pagan Christs*, p. 185.
[2] P. 121, n. 2. This is a mistranslation which Mr. Robertson corrected later. It is the one who offers a sacrifice who must be willing, not the victim.

known to hold good for universally recognized reasons. Now most of the variations in ritual with which we have been dealing are the modes of procedure successively adopted to attain this one end —the apparent willingness of the victim. Mr. Robertson thus arrived at a scheme of development which seemed to him convincing, because it was so logical.

The scheme must be given in full, in Mr. Robertson's own words.

We can infer the probable line of movement all round in the matter of the usages under notice. As thus:

1. Originally a "willing" victim is desiderated: and willingness is secured by a bribe of a period of ease and licence.

2. This kind of victim becoming hard to procure, one "bought with a price" was substituted, as representing a voluntary offering by his owner or owners.

3. Still seeking the semblance of a "willing" sacrifice, the sacrificers first broke the limbs of the human victim.

4. Feeling (on some reformer's urging) that such a mangled victim was an unseemly sacrifice, they resorted to narcotics.

5. At a higher stage of social evolution, recoiling from the sacrifice of an innocent victim, men fell back upon condemned criminals, and these in turn are stupefied, from humane or other motives.

6. Being next persuaded that the stupefied victim was either an unseemly or an inefficacious because non-suffering sacrifice, or being on other grounds inclined to abandon human sacrifice, they substituted the old sacrifice of an animal, giving it in certain cases human attributes, and in others some of the privileges formerly accorded to the *taboo* human victim. In the case of

the animal it was not as a rule felt necessary either to break bones or to use narcotics, though either plan might be used. But reformers would stress the avoidance of bone-breaking by way of showing the superiority of the new sacrifice: hence the need for a veto on imitations of the old practice.[1]

It thus appears that many details of the story of the Cross correspond closely to the various modes employed at different periods and in different rituals to secure the willingness of the victim. By a study of certain other particulars of the gospel-narrative, Mr. Robertson thought he could define yet more clearly the kind of sacrificial rite for which the mystery-drama was substituted.

The parallels so far presented explain why in the myth the divine victim is betrayed and bought for a price, why he receives a narcotic and a spear-thrust, and why the legs of his comrades are broken though his own are carefully kept intact. Another sacrificial clue will enable us to see why he dies as a king, why he is mocked and scourged, why he is tried and degraded. Some time ago Sir James Frazer suggested that " the gospel crucifixion incidentally reproduced the features of a sacrifice of a mock king in the Perso-Babylonian Feast of the Sacaea." " The Jews may have copied from the Babylonians the practice of putting to death (in the Feast of Purim) a malefactor who, after masquerading as Mordecai, in a crown and royal robe, was hanged or crucified in the character of Haman."[2] Readers who wish to follow up this theory must turn to Frazer's *Golden Bough*; but

[1] *Pagan Christs*, p. 156.
[2] *Ibid.*, p. 145.

for weighty reasons to which we may return later, Mr. Robertson rejected it. He believed, however, that Frazer had pointed out the right direction for inquiry. Though not derived from the Sacaea, these features of the gospel-narrative must come from a similar Jewish practice in which a male-factor played the part of a mock-king and was subsequently sacrificed by crucifixion. Two other rites, in Rhodes and Phœnicia, throw a very high light on this Jewish practice. In Rhodes a man was annually sacrificed to the ancient Semitic deity Kronos. "A prisoner condemned to death was selected and kept till the Kronian festival, when he was led outside the city-gates, and, *having been given wine to drink,* put to death. Here we have at length a close parallel in the Mediterranean world to what we have reason to regard as a typical detail in the gospel mystery-play."[1]

Can we get any further light on this most interesting Rhodian ritual? The use of a criminal in the sacrifice is clearly a late development. In the scheme which Mr. Robertson worked out, the use of criminals represents the *fifth* stage of the evolution of human sacrifice. Consequently Mr. Robertson would appear to have been abundantly justified when he said, "The Kronian victim at Rhodes we know cannot have been originally a criminal: and it is much more likely than not that he originally personated either the God Kronos, or, as seems most probable, the 'only begotten son' Ieoud, whom, in a Phœnician myth, Kronos is said to have sacrificed after dressing him in royal robes."[1] This brings us to the Phœnician practice

[1] *Pagan Christs*, p. 137.

and myth, which enables us to reconstruct the original rite, some variant of which was replaced by and embodied in the gospel mystery-drama.

A more extended reference to this myth is to be found on page 161 of *Pagan Christs*, where we learn that " Kronos ' whom the Phœnicians call Israel ' adorned his son Ieoud, ' the only,' with emblems of royalty, and sacrificed him. The actuality of such a belief among the Phœnicians is proved by the story of Maleus crucifying his only son, crowned and robed in purple, before the walls of Carthage, in order to conquer the city. He was fulfilling an august rite." Since the island of Rhodes was much under the influence of Phœnicia, it is fair to assume that the annual sacrifice to Kronos originally resembled the august rite revealed in this myth and carried out by Maleus.

This brings us to another typical reconstruction which also must be given at length in Mr. Robertson's own words. He says:

We have now followed our historic clues far enough to warrant a constructive theory. Indeed, it frames itself when we colligate our main data. As thus:

1. In the slaying of the Kronian victim at Rhodes, we have an ancient Semitic human sacrifice maintained into the historic period, by the expedient of taking as annual victim a criminal already condemned to death.

2. In Semitic mythology, Kronos " whom the Phœnicians call Israel " sacrifices his son Ieoud, " the only," after putting upon him royal robes.

3. The Feast of Kronos is the Saturnalia, in which elsewhere a mock-king plays a prominent part: and as Kronos was among the Semites identified with Moloch = " king," the victim would be ostensibly either a

king or a king's son. A trial and degradation were likely accessories.

4. Supposing the victim in the Rhodian Saturnalia to figure as Ieoud, he would be *ipso facto* Barabbas, " the son of the father," and in the terms of the case he was a condemned criminal. At the same time, in terms of the myth, he would figure in royal robes.

5. In any case, the myth being Semitic, it is morally certain that among the many cases of human sacrifice in the Græco-Semitic world, the Rhodian rite was not unique. And as the name " Ieoud " besides signifying " the only " was ritually identical with the Greek and Hebrew names for Judah (son of " Israel ") and Jew (Yehuda, Ioudaios), it was extremely likely among the Jews of the Dispersion, to be regarded as having special application to their race, which in their sacred books actually figured as the Only-Begotten Son of the Father God, and as having undergone special suffering.

6. That the Rhodian rite, Semitic in origin, was at some points specially coincident with Jewish conceptions of sacrifice, is proved by the detail of leading the prisoner outside the city gates.

This is expressly laid down in the Epistle to the Hebrews, as a ritual condition of the sacrificial death of Jesus.[1]

Thus it would seem that Mr. Robertson patiently and laboriously rediscovered an ancient Semitic sacrifice in which the victim was regarded as the only-begotten son of a divine racial father and in which the victim perishes as a king. *This is precisely the case presented by the Christian story of the Cross.*

Mr. Robertson was careful not to claim an exact parallel. He recognized that on the evidence this

[1] *Pagan Christs*, p. 186 f.

Rhodian rite differs from the rite underlying the gospel-narratives in two important respects, first in date, the crucifixion being assigned to the time of the Passover (March), while the Rhodian Saturnalia was a June or July Festival: and second in this, that " there is no hint of a triple execution." But he thought he was justified in believing that a variant of the Rhodian rite, an annual sacrifice of Ieoud or Barabbas must have been current among the Jews somewhere and sometime, and like the Rhodian rite must have been transformed into a mystery-play. The coincidence of detail between the story of the Cross and this ancient Semitic ritual of human sacrifice seemed to Mr. Robertson too close to admit of any reasonable doubt.

Since some readers may be bewildered by the succession of details in this chapter, a very brief recapitulation may be of service. According to Mr. Robertson, the following features in the gospel-story have been discovered in different forms of human sacrifice: the betrayal for money, the trial and degradation of a mock-king, the use of a narcotic, the draught of wine (two items unnecessarily separated in the gospels), the breaking of the legs, the spear-thrust, the royal dignity attributed to the sufferer, and above all the custom of regarding the sufferer as the only-begotten son of the Father!

All these important elements in the gospel-story of the Cross are links in the chain of evidence which points to a human sacrifice as the basis of the Christian mystery-play.

CHAPTER VI

DOUBTS AND QUESTIONS CONCERNING THE SACRI-
FICIAL BASIS OF THE STORY OF THE CRUCIFIXION

In outlining Mr. Robertson's attempt to discover
the source of the gospel mystery-drama in a
primitive rite of human sacrifice, we hinted at
certain difficulties which were disclosed by the
very statement of his theory. The more leisurely
consideration of the contents of the preceding
chapter, on which we now enter, will demonstrate
that the difficulties involved are really insuperable. The evidence adduced by Mr. Robertson
does not suffice to prove his case, even if we could
accept his interpretation of it. But as we shall
discover, again and again Mr. Robertson read
into his facts and quotations what he wanted to
find there, and when put into the witness-box
and cross-examined, his witnesses let him down
and turn against him.

Let us take first the endeavour to find a historic
instance of the transition from a genuine sacrifice
to a mock-sacrifice or a mystery-drama, which Mr.
Robertson's theory requires. The instance offered
to us is the sacrifice in Rhodes.[1] We are told

[1] p. 187.

that Porphyry casually and simply remarks that this particular rite was changed. The nature of the change is not further specified, and this leaves room for conjecture. Accepting this statement as it stands, there is nothing convincing about the particular conjecture which Mr. Robertson favoured. A mock-sacrifice or a mystery-drama are mentioned as the only likely alternatives. Yet there are other possible changes, and on Mr. Robertson's own scheme of the all-round evolution of human sacrifice, the most obvious and probable change is the substitution of an animal for a man. It follows that we are not obliged to adopt either of his suggested alternatives. However, the probable meaning, if not the plain sense of the passage of Porphyry, leaves little or no room for any conjecture. *Porphyry actually says what the change was.* The innovation consisted in substituting a criminal condemned to death for an innocent victim.[1] As this is the only example cited of the assumed transition from sacrifice to drama,

---

[1] The passage from Porphyry may be found in the original Greek in Eusebius, *Præparatio Evangelica,* Book IV, Chapter XVI. It may be Englished thus: " For in Rhodes also in the month Metageitnion (= mid-August to mid-September) on the sixth day of the month, a man used to be sacrificed to Kronos. Which custom having prevailed for a long period was changed: for they kept in custody a criminal who had been condemned to death, until the festival of Kronos, and when the festival had begun (or perhaps, when the festival was at hand) they led the man outside the gates directly opposite the abode of Aristoboule and having given him wine to drink, they slaughtered him."

It is possible to take the sentence, " for they kept in custody . . ." as descriptive of the ancient custom; but it is more naturally taken as descriptive of the change. Cf. J. G. Frazer, *The Scapegoat,* p. 354.

the external evidence vanishes. We do not know that such a transition ever took place any-where. But, of course, the parallels adduced to various particulars in the gospel-narratives, may rehabilitate the thesis.

Mr. Robertson had an extraordinary eye for parallels. He lighted on the most unsuspected parallels with amazing quickness, but unfor-tunately the parallels were often forced and unreal. In many instances, the more superficial the resemblance, the more Mr. Robertson seemed to be impressed by it. We may take three ex-amples, two of which we have already recorded in the previous chapter, and the other of which we shall add, since it is underlined, so to speak, in *Pagan Christs,* as forming a singularly sug-gestive parallel. The first example is the spear-thrust. The Albanians used to slay an anointed victim by thrusting a sacred lance through his side, and then they would draw auguries from the manner of his fall.[1] "This is a sacrifice corres-ponding in one notable detail, etc." Now the extent of the correspondence is just the bare fact of a spear-thrust in the side—a fact which in itself has no sacrificial significance whatever. What makes the deed sacrificial in the Albanian case is that the blow is delivered with a *sacred* spear, is mortal and intended to consummate the sacrifice, and finally provides omens. *All the features which make the detail sacrificial in the Albanian instance are wanting in the gospels.* The spear is not sacred, the blow is not mortal, it does not consummate the sacrifice, it has no

[1] p. 125.

sacrificial purpose. A more superficial resemblance it would be difficult to conceive. Nor is
this all; if the detail in the gospels be sacrificial,
it does not come from a ritual of crucifixion or
of quasi-crucifixion or from some *similar* ritual,
as Mr. Robertson supposed. The kind of ritual
to which such a method of ceremonial slaying
belongs, e.g. the Albanian ritual, is as unlike a
crucifixion as any human sacrifice could be. The
spear-thrust has no place in the primitive rite
as last performed, and on Mr. Robertson's hypothesis, its introduction into the gospel-drama is
unintelligible.

The second example is the use Mr. Robertson
made of the rite of triple sacrifice at Bundair in
Jeypore. In his last book, *Jesus and Judas*,[1] he
wrote: "We know now that in certain ancient
human sacrifices the special victim was placed
between two others." The only evidence adduced
for this is the sacrifice to the Sun-god at one
festival of three victims, "one at the east, one at
the west, and the third in the centre of the
village."[2] The three victims are treated exactly
alike, and except for the number, there is not the
faintest resemblance between this triple sacrifice
and the execution of Jesus between two thieves.
We do not know of more than one ancient sacrifice
involving three victims. In the one case cited we
do not know that any one of the three was regarded
as the special victim, and if there was a special
victim we do not know that he was placed between
two others. There is no reason for thinking that

[1] Op. cit., p. 52.
[2] *Pagan Christs*, p. 115.

the triple execution recorded in the gospels is, or could be, derived from any sacrificial ritual. The attempt to find a sacrificial origin for the triple execution makes hopeless nonsense of the rest of Mr. Robertson's theory.

The third example is given in this sentence about the Khonds and their rite of human sacrifice. "Their placing of the victim, for instance, on a cross, or in a cleft bough in such a way as to make a living cross, wherein the God is, as it were, part of the living tree, is a singularly suggestive parallel."[1]

The two alternative methods of dispatching the victim, to which Mr. Robertson referred, he described on an earlier page, where he said, "Finally (the victim) was either fastened to a cross, of which the horizontal bar, pierced by the upright, could be raised or lowered at will, or placed in the cleft or split made in a long branch of a green tree, which was made to grasp his neck or chest, the open ends being closed or tightly tied, so as to imprison him in the wood and make, as it were, a cross, of which he was the upright." . . .[2]

Mr. Robertson's authority for the first method was his own study of a photograph of a sacrifice post, published by Mr. Thurston.[3] The second method is detailed at length by those from whom we derive our information as to the Meriah sacrifice among the Khonds.

It is worth noting that Mr. Robertson here put

[1] *Pagan Christs*, p. 118.
[2] Ibid., p. 113.
[3] *Castes and Tribes in Southern India*, III, p. 377.

73

forward with equal confidence and as of equal
evidential value, a description of the Khonds'
procedure which rested simply on his own conjecture, and a description embodying the testimony of eye-witnesses. No first-hand observer
ever found the Khonds fastening the victim to
a cross, or raising and lowering him on a cross-bar.
As a matter of fact, Mr. Robertson's conjectural
interpretation of Mr. Thurston's photograph is
entirely unsupported. The post was not used as
a cross, and there is no cross-bar. In 1917, the
curator of the Government Museum at Madras,
where this relic is preserved, wrote to me as
follows: "The part of the Meriah-post which
you refer to as the cross-bar, was originally
shaped like the head of an elephant, the trunk
to which the victim was tied being the part which
hangs down on the extreme right of the photograph." The victim was tied to the trunk, and
whirled round in the air. This is not even quasi-
crucifixion. The first suggestive parallel existed
only in Mr. Robertson's imagination, and it
reveals the dangerous obsession with which he
approached the whole inquiry.[1]

The worth of the resemblance which Mr.
Robertson detected in the normal and well-
attested method of sacrifice among the Khonds,
will be apparent if we recall the description of
the rite given by Major Macpherson. At a given
spot, selected overnight, "a short post is inserted.
Around it four larger posts are usually set up, and

[1] In this instance, Mr. Robertson readily acknowledged his
mistake and retracted his statement. See *The Jesus-Problem*,
p. 62 n. He still maintained that "the Dravidian victim, the
deified sacrifice, was *as-it-were* crucified."

in the midst of these the victim is placed. The priest, assisted by the chief and one or two of the elders, now takes the branch of a green tree cleft several feet down the centre. They insert the victim between the rift, fitting it in some districts to his chest, in others to his throat. Cords are then twisted round the open extremity of the stake, which the priest, aided by his assistants, strives with his whole force to close; he then wounds the victim slightly with his axe, when the crowd throws itself upon the sacrifice, and strips the flesh from the bones." . . .

To this horrible process Mr. Robertson alluded when he spoke of placing the victim (in a cleft bough) " in such a way as to make a living cross, wherein the god is, as it were, part of the living tree," or when he said that the open ends of the bough were tightly tied "so as to imprison the victim in the wood, and make as it were a cross, of which he was the upright." These phrases convey the suggestion that the *purpose* of so treating the victim was to make him form a cross, and make him appear as part of the living tree, but no such purpose can be traced in the rite as described by Major Macpherson. The green bough is used for obvious practical reasons. A dry bough would crack. There is no intention of making the god part of a living tree. If the victim did present a superficial cruciform appearance—and he may have done so—this is a purely accidental feature of the Khond ritual, one which had no interest for the Khonds themselves. It had no sacrificial significance. The Khonds' method of dispatching their victim was not a

crucifixion, and did not distantly resemble a
crucifixion. The parallel under discussion is
indeed suggestive. It suggests the extraordinary
ease with which Mr. Robertson convinced himself he had found a parallel.

The degraded rite practised among the Khonds
might conceivably be included under that con-
veniently elastic term "quasi-crucifixion"; but
it is a singular fact that the Rhodian rite and the
sacrifice presupposed by the Phœnician myth of
Kronos and Ieoud—the two sacrifices which are
held to furnish the type to which the Palestinian
rite belongs—are neither of them rites of crucifixion at all.

The Rhodian victim is simply slaughtered, the
Greek word which I translated, "they slaughtered
him," implying that he had his throat cut, or was
dispatched by the knife in some way. Ieoud is
represented as sacrificed on an altar, no doubt, by
knife and fire. So, if the Jews did practise a
parallel ritual of human sacrifice, it certainly
would not have been a rite of crucifixion. The
gospel-narratives cannot be based on a variant of
the type of ancient Semitic sacrifice, which Mr.
Robertson discovered in Rhodes and Phœnicia.
For that type, if it exist, differs fundamentally
from any rite of crucifixion.

It is also rather strange that Mr. Robertson,
who was so careful to point out that the Rhodian
sacrifice differs from his imagined Palestinian rite,
in two particulars—the date and the number of
victims—omitted to draw attention to this fundamental difference in the way the sacrifice is con-
summated. Readers ought to have been told that

Mr. Robertson was deriving the story of the cross from a ritual in which there was no cross.

But perhaps we are going too fast, for is there not the clear instance of Maleus crucifying his son in purple before the walls of Carthage? Is not this the august rite in being?

This particular case is worth examining, as it exhibits in a marked degree Mr. Robertson's power of reading into the evidence what he wanted to find in it, without any warrant, and even against the express tenor of the passage he was citing.[1] The story of Maleus in the historian Justin, is as follows:

Maleus, a dishonoured general, is besieging Carthage, in order to get reinstated. His siege is not very successful. His son, Carthalo, has gone over or remained loyal to the other side. One day Carthalo comes into camp, dressed in the purple robe and fillets of a priest (i.e. he comes with the safeguard of a sacred envoy). The father loses his temper, regards him as a traitor and a spy, and " so bade fix him and his ornaments to a very high cross in the sight of the city." *There is not a trace of sacrifice or august ritual in the story from beginning to end.*

I had the advantage of discussing this particular point with Mr. Robertson in 1917, and he dealt with it in a letter which I value because it reveals at once the candour and courtesy with which he would discuss difficulties in private correspondence, and the ease with which he substituted his own or other people's inferences for the actual statements of the authorities he was quoting.

[1] p. 161.

"The Justin passage seems to have been twice dealt with by me, first in Note 4, where the point is simply 'King's son.' (I have an instance from New Zealand, where 'Chief's son' has the same virtue.) The 'only son' passage seems to have been inserted in the text by me afterwards—apparently on some other suggestion. You are quite right as to the text of Justin, which does not say 'only son.' The son is 'dressed in purple and fillets of a priest,' or again, 'dressed in purple and gold.' And 'So he bade fix him and his ornaments to a very high cross in the sight of the city.' I rather suspect that some author whom I was following had inferred that Justin misunderstood the nature of the episode, since the historic point is that 'A few days after that he captured Carthage.' But I will have to investigate afresh. These are old studies with me, and for most of the last ten years I have been occupied with other matters. I notice that some codices have for Maleus *Malcheus,* and that Cortius in his edition has *Malchus.* As this means 'King,' the inference has probably been drawn that the sacrifice was regal. But I cannot now recall the author that may have discussed the point. In any case, the special value of the regal sacrifice is certain." The possibility that the general was named Malchus is interesting, though it does not justify the assumption that he and his son were of royal rank. General King is not necessarily an actual King![1] It remains true that in the original text of Justin there is no hint of an "only son,"

[1] In John xviii. 10 Malchus is the name of a slave of the high priest.

no suggestion of a kingly crown or royal robes, and no mention of a sacrifice, though this ruthless execution may have appeared as a dread sacrifice to the Carthaginians who suffered defeat or surrendered.

So far as our inquiry has gone, we have found no certain instance of a drama based upon a ritual of human sacrifice or substituted for it. We have found no certain instance of crucifixion as a mode of human sacrifice. If the rite on which the drama was based, the rite as last publicly performed, was a rite of crucifixion, we have observed that there could be no place in such a rite for the use of a spear as in the Albanian, and that there is no parallel as yet to the sacrifice of the special victim between two others. Mr. Robertson accounted neither for the cross nor for the spear-thrust, nor for the presence of the two robbers.

CHAPTER VII

STRANGE SPECULATIONS REGARDING HUMAN SACRIFICE

BEFORE we attempt a final estimate of the supposed connection between the story of the Cross and a rite of human sacrifice with many variants, it is necessary to examine a little more closely the two studies in the history of human sacrifice which form an essential part of Mr. Robertson's argument.

The first is the scheme of evolution whereby certain usages in relation to human sacrifice are supposed to have succeeded one another. The prime necessity being a willing victim, the unhappy wretch was (1) first bribed with a year's licence, and then when bribes failed (2) a victim bought with a price was substituted. Since the willingness of the seller did not always ensure the willingness of the person sold (3) the practice of leg-breaking was introduced to prevent resistance. This was followed by (4) the use of a narcotic, and natural transitions led to the use first of criminals (5) and lastly of animals (6).

Here, then, we have an orderly and convincing development. And, strange to say, all these stages, which succeed and supplant one another, are, with the exception of the last, found to co-exist in the gospels. The purchase with a price, the leg-breaking, the use of narcotics, the use of criminals—all these features marked the primitive rite as last performed in public. And yet *ex hypothesi*, if stupefied criminals were being used, if the fifth stage had been reached, the leg-breaking and the purchase with a price must have fallen out of use.

If Mr. Robertson had really traced a genuine evolution, he could not fairly ask us to believe that all these items existed together in a single Palestinian rite, or even in a number of variants, since the practices in question belong to different stages of culture.

It is true that these earlier practices when no longer used need not have been forgotten. The tenacity of folk-memory opens a way to rehabilitate Mr. Robertson's argument. Let us revise his thesis, and base the gospel-narrative not on a drama, but on a pageant of human sacrifice! This hypothesis will really meet the whole case. It will explain why the story of the Cross is such an amazing epitome of sacrificial usage from the barbarous ritual of the Khonds to the more refined practice of the Passover. Some enterprising forerunner of Mr. Louis Parker, observing the immense vogue of human sacrifice in the Mediterranean world and the hankering of the Jews after all sorts of sacrifice, must have hit the public taste with a pageant that was a marvel of anthropological research.

Without waiting to develop this suggestion, let us turn to another serious difficulty which this scheme of evolution creates for the original hypothesis. Mr. Robertson discovered traces of the first stage—the most primitive practice of a bribe by licence—in the one year's duration of the ministry, and in the association of the Messiah with harlots. He even added that the ascription of the title " Nazarite " to Jesus may be explained by assuming that the Jewish victim, like the Khond, wore his hair unshorn.[1] Let us assume the discoveries, and then ask how it comes that all these sacrificial features appear in the earlier matter of the gospels, in those parts of the gospels which Mr. Robertson indignantly denied[2] that he ever thought of deriving from a drama based on human sacrifice? How did the picture of the sacrificial victim consorting with harlots find its way into the Primitive Gospel which has no story of the crucifixion and which is apparently to be regarded as the work of Judaic Jesuists who had not the Christian doctrine of a divine sacrifice? Mr. Robertson seems to have been involved in the following dilemma. If he was right in asserting that these features of the earlier chapters of the gospels are sacrificial, if the friendship with sinners expressly mentioned in the Primitive Gospel really reflects primitive sacrificial usage as practised among Khonds and Aztecs, then the story of the Cross cannot be an afterthought. The account of the sacrifice cannot have been added on later. The Primitive Gospel cannot have ended without a Passion-story. So if these discoveries were correct, Mr. Robertson was effectively destroying his original starting-point.

[1] The title " Nazarite " is nowhere applied to Jesus. Without any justification, Mr. Robertson assumed that the words Nazarene and Nazoroean which are applied to Jesus in the New Testament are equivalent to Nazarite or Nazirite.
[2] In reply to Father Martindale. *Pagan Christs*, p. 414.

The narrative of the Cross can never have stood alone. It was led up to by the scheme of the ministry, by the long hair implied in the term Nazarite and so on. On the other hand, if Mr. Robertson was not prepared to surrender his starting-point, he should have abandoned his discoveries. He should have maintained at all costs that these features were not sacrificial, because they did not belong to the mystery-drama which was added to the Primitive Gospel.

There appears, however, to be an easy way to evade or minimize at least the first of these difficulties, and that is, to recognize that the probable line of movement traced for us by Mr. Robertson is purely arbitrary and artificial. The scheme of evolution, logical and attractive as it is, falls to pieces on closer examination. To begin with, it is not, strictly speaking, an evolution at all. The stages marked out are not really successive and do not depend on one another. Among the Khonds the first two practices, the year's licence, and the purchase of victims, went on side by side up to the last, and were combined successively with limb-breaking and the use of opium. There is no reason to suppose limb-breaking to be a later practice than purchase, nor purchase a later practice than licence. They are not three different practices successively adopted to secure the same end, a willing victim, but three different practices simultaneously employed to secure different ends. On the other hand the use of a criminal is a genuine transition which *ipso facto* excludes the second stage, the purchase of a victim. Similarly the use of a narcotic might supersede the third stage, the limb-breaking. But the first four stages are not real stages, leading up to the fifth, the use of a criminal. Nor does the transition to this latter stage, when discovered in history, justify one in assuming that the previous four stages must have been traversed in order to reach it. For example, when we find a criminal sacrificed in Rhodes, we have no right to assume that previously the victim was bribed by a year's licence, or bought with a price, or subjected to leg-breaking. The whole alleged evolution is a sham.

This will appear evident from another consideration. The so-called stages are not held together by an inner principle. Mr. Robertson essayed to link them, as a series of practices intended to secure a willing victim. But it is not immediately obvious that the usages which Mr. Robertson here grouped together were so many attempts to secure this desired end.

Stage (2), the purchase of a victim from a willing seller, may be dismissed at once. It clearly has nothing to do with the willingness of the victim, nor is there any logical transition from (2) to (3), from purchase to leg-breaking. Again, there is not much ground for treating the period of licence as a bribe. It may have been partly that, but it may have been maintained and was probably initiated for quite other reasons—primarily out of respect to the god's representative, and out of the desire to secure supposed blessings from his wayward activity. Again, it is not clear that the breaking of the legs was employed as a device to create the semblance of willingness. Major Macpherson, describing the Khond sacrifice, does indeed say,

" As the victim must not suffer bound, nor on the other hand make any show of resistance, the bones of his arms and if necessary those of his legs are sometimes broken." But I cannot see that this implies, as Mr. Robertson imagines, an attempt to make the victim appear to be a willing offering to the god. The bones are broken that the victim may not resist those who are hacking him to pieces, just as he must remain unbound in order that the people may get at him. In the case of the Khonds, the custom of leg-breaking is adopted for severely practical reasons. It is not clear that leg-breaking ever anywhere had anything to do with securing the willingness or quasi-willingness of the victim. However, it is sufficient for our purpose to note that the usages which Mr. Robertson strung together as stages of an evolution are not really linked by one psychological principle such as the desire to make the victim appear willing.

That the evolution is a sham, that the stages are for the most part not real successive stages at all, and that the thread by which it is proposed to hold them together is too weak for the purpose—these are perhaps the most serious, but not the only, defects in this at first sight attractive piece of theoretical reconstruction. There are others.

It is surely strange that what is offered as the probable line of movement all round has not been shown to be the actual line of movement anywhere. Mr. Robertson enunciated a general law without the support of a single instance. He could show the first four stages existing or rather co-existing among the Khonds. He could trace one or other of them among different barbarous peoples. Similarly,

he could point to stages (4) and (5) co-existing in
Rhodes. What cannot be discovered, is any
instance which brings the earlier and later stages of
his scheme together. Of course there are instances
on record in which the use of a criminal supersedes
an earlier form of sacrifice in which the victim was
not a criminal, and these may suffice to establish a
general law of development. But Mr. Robertson
did not produce any instance of the criminal super-
seding the victim bought with a price, and he did
not show any inner necessity for such a supersession.
Least of all could he show that where you have the
criminal, you may be sure you once had the victim
bought with a price. What Mr. Robertson did was
first to trace certain practices among the Khonds
and certain other practices among more civilized
peoples, and then to link these together by an
arbitrary and unsatisfactory principle. On the
strength of this fanciful connection, he claimed the
right to assume that " among some of the more
civilized peoples of the Mediterranean, similar pro-
cesses (to the bogus-evolution which Mr. Robertson
discovers among the Khonds, stages (1) to (4)) had
been sometimes gone through about two thousand
years ago."[1]

No scientific anthropologist would take such a
reconstruction seriously. To treat this arbitrary
scheme of development as the probable line of
movement all round, is absurd. To assume it for
the Mediterranean world, and to label it, as Mr.
Robertson did, " the Judaic evolution," would
be regarded as impertinence in any writer less
sincere.

[1] p. 121.

But note what follows. This sorry scheme of evolution cannot be restored, and yet, only if it be true, only if the usages discussed are closely linked together, was Mr. Robertson justified in his constant appeal to savage peoples. His parallels from the Khonds and others are worthless, because they are only relevant if the usages concerned form part of a general scheme of development to which the history of human sacrifice among the Jews and Mediterranean peoples may be presumed to have conformed. Trained anthropologists are sceptical as to the existence of any such general law of development. There is no reason to suppose that the institution of human sacrifice developed in the same way in the Mediterranean world and in Mexico, or even followed the same line among such closely connected peoples as the Phœnicians and the Jews. But only if there be such a general law, and only if the scheme of evolution we have been examining embodies that law, have we the right to assume without positive evidence that at some time or other the Jews must have bribed their victims with a year's licence or bought them with a price. Of course, even if Mr. Robertson's scheme of development were true, we could not assume, as he did, without evidence, that the development took place among some of the more civilized Mediterranean peoples *about 2000 years ago*. But since the whole scheme cannot be called an evolution even by courtesy, since the items are only artificially linked, and fall apart on analysis, Mr. Robertson's whole procedure in citing barbaric practices is invalidated. The details in the crucifixion which he parallels from the Khonds and other barbarians have not thereby been proved to be sacrificial for any Mediterranean people. The main argument in short simply disappears.

CHAPTER VIII

FURTHER STRANGE SPECULATIONS REGARDING HUMAN SACRIFICE

It is no light matter to take to pieces Mr. Robertson's elaborate but unsubstantial chains of inference. But we cannot pass by his second attempt at constructive theory. We have given verbatim the long passage in which he put together the known facts of the Rhodian rite, the sacrifice implied in the myth of Kronos and Ieoud, and certain features of Saturnalia outside Rhodes. He thus evolved a rite very like the crucifixion. It is interesting to observe how the likeness is obtained.

The Rhodian rite is taken as the basis, and fresh details are crowded into Porphyry's meagre reference, until Mr. Robertson has built up a sacrifice closely resembling the Palestinian rite of which we are in search. First, the Kronian victim at Rhodes is supposed to personate Ieoud of the Phœnician story. Sir James Frazer suggested that the victim may have stood for Kronos; but no— Mr. Robertson assures us it is most probable that he personated Ieoud. Why is it most probable? Well, Phœnicia influenced Rhodes and so we may at once identify the annual public sacrifice of a man to Kronos at Rhodes with the occasional sacrifice of a scion of the royal house at a time of crisis in Phœnicia (the kind of sacrifice at which the myth hints). There is in reality no reason whatever for connecting the Phœnician myth with the Rhodian rite. Mr. Robertson's theory of probability is very clear and simple. That is " most probable," which is most convenient for his theory. The same notion of probability underlies the sentence, " A trial and degradation were *likely* accessories." There is no evidence of a trial and degradation in connection either with the Phœnician myth or the Rhodian sacrifice. A trial and degradation would be quite out of place in the august ritual in which the king's son is sacrificed in full regalia, and consequently if Mr. Robertson was right in identifying the Kronian victim with Ieoud, the trial and degradation would be equally out of place in the Rhodian rite. If there is anything to be said for his first most probable identification, it compels us to discard his likely accessories. But both likelihoods derive from a biased imagination, and are adopted, without evidence, to suggest some sort of resemblance to the Christian story.

But, it may be said, surely a trial and degradation might be associated with the mock-king of the Saturnalia? This is true, but unfortunately, we have no ground for transferring to Rhodes, features of the Saturnalia at Rome or of the Sacaea at Babylon. Mr. Robertson criticized Sir James Frazer for trying to connect the Sacaea, a New Year's festival, with Purim which falls in March. Then why did he forget his excellent critical

principles and himself transfer to the festival of
Kronos held in Rhodes in August-September,
features of the New Year festivals of Rome and
Babylon? But apart from this, if we assume that
a mock-king plays a prominent part in the festival
of Kronos at Rhodes, the victim of the ritual
described by Porphyry can scarcely have been the
man. For he is led out to die "*when the feast has
begun!*" (i.e. towards the beginning of the feast),
whereas the mock-king reigns through the festival.
So it is hazardous to connect any features of the
Sacaea or Saturnalia with the Kronian victim in
Rhodes.

There is one other feature of this second study
which calls for brief examination. Mr. Robertson proposed to bring this sacrifice of Ieoud by
Kronos on to Palestinian soil, by identifying
Kronos with Israel, and Ieoud with Judah (son of
"Israel"). The suggestion is that in earlier myth
Israel may have sacrificed Judah just as Kronos
sacrificed Ieoud, or at least that Jews of the Dispersion, finding the sacrifice of Ieoud by Kronos
"whom the Phœnicians called Israel" in existence
at Rhodes, would regard it with special interest as
applying to their race and their patriarch "Judah."

There are certain difficulties in this theory,
beyond the difficulty we have already noticed, viz.
that there is no reason to suppose the Kronian
victim at Rhodes to have been called Ieoud or
Barabbas at all. But to begin with, Israel or Jacob
would seem to be precluded from emulating
Kronos, by the mere size of his family. The father
of twelve sons could hardly have sacrificed an
"only-begotten" son even in a myth, and Judah is

not even the first-born! The rôle of Kronos and Ieoud cannot be transferred to Israel and Judah.

In the second place, the phrase to which Mr. Robertson appealed, which he repeated with evident satisfaction and on which his argument depends—the phrase, " Kronos whom the Phœnicians call Israel "—is the reading of some inferior manuscripts, and is certainly not the true text of Eusebius, the authority he is citing. The Phœnicians did not call Kronos Israel; they called him " El." There is no doubt as to the correct tradition. Not only does Gaisford in his edition of Eusebius, *Præparatio Evangelica*, edit Ēlos or Ilos in the text in the passages which Mr. Robertson is quoting, but an earlier passage, which shows no variant, tells us " the allies of El, that is, Kronos, are called Elohim." (Eus., op. cit. I. 10.) The true tradition is independently reported in a comment of Servius on the Aeneid, where again the Phœnicians call Kronos El, not Israel. So Mr. Robertson's main contention rested on a copyist's error that had long ago been corrected. Unless we are prepared to treat an obvious blunder of a monastic scribe as a serious historical authority, we have no evidence at all to connect Kronos and Israel.

One further difficulty may be mentioned. Neither in Greek nor in Hebrew are the words Je-oud and Judah or Jew virtually identical. Since Je-oud means " only " or " only-begotten," it is connected with the Hebrew word Yachid, which has that meaning. The Hebrew word for Judah and Jew which Mr. Robertson transliterates Yehuda, means " praise." If by any chance some Jews did connect Je-oud with Judah, it is not likely

that they took Je-oud to mean " only-begotten."
Judah is normally and rightly explained as meaning " praise." There is one passage where a com-
mentator on the book of Esther connects the word
Jew with the root Yachid. We are told that
Mordecai was called a Jew " because he insisted
on the unity of God (unified the name of the
Holy One, Blessed is He!)." Even in this instance
there is no trace of the Phœnician Je-oud.

We may now leave the details of these colliga-
tions of data, and look at the impossibilities of the
general result. It has already been suggested that
Mr. Robertson's argument leads up to a sacrifice
embracing details which could not have co-existed
in the same ritual. This difficulty is relieved by
positing variants of this ritual of crucifixion or
quasi-crucifixion. Thus the leg-breaking belongs
to a variant in which the crucifixion did not involve
the nailing of the feet. The spear-thrust is derived
from an entirely alien ritual in which the victim
was not crucified at all. Of course, the multiplica-
tion of variants and other non-crucifixion rituals
intensifies the difficulty which we have yet to face—
the difficulty of believing that any of these variants
were practised in Palestine about 2,000 years ago.
The greater the number of variants, i.e. of distinct
sacrifices, which the theory requires to have been
current together, the more damning is the fact that
we have no positive evidence of the practice of any
of them. They cannot all have escaped notice.
But in any case when Mr. Robertson had unloaded
all he could on to variants and quite alien rituals,
he was still left with an impossibly hybrid rite
which could never at any period of human history

have been performed, though, as I have said, the story might arise out of a telescoped pageant reviewing the whole history of human sacrifice.

Mr. Robertson assumed that the victims were malefactors. It follows, then, on his own theory, and in the nature of the case, that the victims could not have been " bought with a price." Consequently the Betrayal, as Mr. Robertson interprets it, cannot belong to the same ritual as the crucifixion itself. Nor will it do to say one victim was " bought with a price " and the others were malefactors. For all three were executed as malefactors, and the two practices cannot be combined. For on Mr. Robertson's own showing, the use of criminals comes in when men are civilized enough to revolt from the use of innocent victims bought with a price. The Jews can scarcely have been at one and the same time so far civilized as to insist on substituting two criminals for two victims out of three, and so conservative as to insist on retaining the old inhuman system for the third.

Again Mr. Robertson would have us believe first, that the crucifixion was an august ritual in which the victim perished in royal robes as the only-begotten son of a king. At the same time, the whole procedure was a mock-sacrifice, in which the victim is tried and degraded as we may imagine the Saturnalian king to have been, and in which the victim dies without any royal robes. Now the crucifixion cannot have been at one and the same time, the solemn offering up of the dearest emblem of royalty, and the practically non-sacrificial execution of the poor mock-king of the Saturnalia, nor can the victim have perished at once with royal robes and without them. And yet this is what Mr. Robertson's theory demands. Mr. Robertson did not and could not offer us any consistent picture of the primitive rite as last performed.

In a footnote on page 148, Mr. Robertson gave a halting approval to Mr. Lang's criticism of Frazer's theory of the crucifixion, which " turns on the fact that it (Frazer's theory) seeks to combine a great many disparate sacrificial motives. This is not absolutely an effective objection, in as much as religion is full of inconsistencies: but Dr. Frazer imputes too much power of combination to a given cult. Popular sacrifice must clearly subsist on a simple basis." What, then, are we to say of Mr. Robertson's theory, which proposes to combine in one rite, the divergent practices and motives (1) of the very primitive and degraded Khonds, (2) of the annual sacrifice of a criminal to Kronos in Rhodes, (3) of the custom of sacrificing children, especially royal children at times of crisis, which once prevailed in Phœnicia, and (4) of the entirely disparate treatment of the mock-king in the Saturnalia? The rite of human sacrifice suggested by Mr. Robertson as the basis of the crucifixion-myth, cannot have been the rite as last publicly performed. Indeed it cannot have been performed anywhere at any time.

CHAPTER IX

HOW MR. ROBERTSON IN HIS SEARCH FOR THE ANCIENT PALESTINIAN RITE REFUTED HIS FIRST THESIS

It must be confessed that it is very difficult to get a clear and convincing idea of the ancient Palestinian rite in which the annual victim was " Jesus, the Son of the Father." It resembles Hamlet's cloud which was at one moment like a camel and at another very like a weasel though at the same time backed like a whale. We must not suspect Mr. Robertson of fooling his readers to the top of their bent, but he was certainly sending them on a fool's errand. No doubt he intended his thesis to be taken seriously, but the more closely it is examined, the more fantastic and incredible it turns out to be.

He offered us four incompatible clues, and if we follow up each in turn, we reach a different conclusion regarding the character of the primitive rite as last publicly performed and regarding the relation of it to the mystery-drama supposedly embodied in the concluding chapters of Matthew or Mark.

There can be little doubt that when he set out to collect parallels to the details of the crucifixion-myth from sacrificial usages, Mr. Robertson hoped that the story as it stood in Matthew would reveal a close approximation to an actual or at least to a conceivable rite of human sacrifice. As his researches developed, that hope receded. The mystery-drama transcribed and added to the Christian gospel does not perpetuate the ancient Palestinian rite. For that we must look to an earlier and much simpler mystery-drama which consisted only of the Supper, the death and the Resurrection.[1] The actual drama now found in the gospels is an elaboration in two or three stages by Gentile hands, and it is very hard to determine which features of it point to certain verifiable details of the original sacrifice. We must then follow up each clue in turn and trace the connection, if any, between the story of the Cross and the rite as last publicly performed.

The parallel with the Khonds is vital, because this is the only example which associates a meal with the sacrifice. According to Mr. Rylands, who at this point is in sympathy with Mr. Robertson, the Last Supper was not the Passover, but a sacrificial meal which points back to a rite wherein the sacrificed victim was actually devoured. "Originally the meal came after the sacrifice."[2] If, then, the mystery-drama perpetuated at bottom the rite as last publicly performed, it should have consisted of two scenes only, the sacrificial death of the victim followed by the sacramental meal.

---

[1] See *The Jesus-Problem*, p. 105.
[2] *Did Jesus Ever Live?* p. 47.

Even the much simpler mystery-drama, consisting of the Supper, the death and the Resurrection is not simple enough. If it really perpetuated the rite as last performed, it should have had no burial and Resurrection scenes and the order of the Supper and the death should have been reversed. From this starting-point we must ask ourselves, what details in the crucifixion-story can be verified as sacrificial? Apart from the Supper itself, the Betrayal scene is most likely to be primitive, since it represents the practice of the Khonds who bought their victims with a price. In that case the three malefactors belong to another and later variant. The leg-breaking and the drugged wine, the narcotic, may, however, be primitive, and possibly the spear-thrust. The only other detail that may be assigned to the original rite is the description of Jesus as a Nazirite. Nothing else can be confidently claimed as belonging to the rite as last performed.

If the ancient ritual was associated with a symbolic meal representing an actual cannibal sacrament, it is practically certain that crucifixion was not the mode of consummating the sacrifice. Mr. Robertson did indeed assert that "in the ritual of the Khonds the symbol of the Cross is prominent in the fashion of slaying the victim," but we know now that his assertion had no basis in fact, and that there is no hint even of quasi-crucifixion in the Meriah-sacrifice. Mr. Rylands has pointed out that the crucifixion does not correspond closely to the interpretation of the death of Christ as a sacrifice, given in the New Testament. He is thinking of references to the redeeming blood of Jesus. " As a matter of fact, hardly any blood can have been shed in the crucifixion as described."[1] We may carry this a stage further. It is clear that the crucifixion as described does not reflect and lead up to a sacrament which speaks not only of bloodshed, but also of a body broken. The description of the crucifixion in John is apparently influenced by the desire to bring out the parallel between Christ and the Paschal Lamb. But conceived as a sacrificial rite, the crucifixion does not fit into the requirement of the sacrificial meal. In the primitive rite, the victim must have been torn or hacked to pieces, and this should have reflected on the mystery-drama and in the myth, as it is in the cults of Attis, Dionysus and Osiris. If the Palestinian rite resembled that of the Khonds, and if the Last Supper was the symbolic representation of a cannibal sacrament, then it is certain that the crucifixion had no place in the last performance of this strange ritual. The victim may have been bought with a price, or he may have been a condemned criminal. He may have been drugged, and he may have had his legs broken. He may have been dispatched with a spear-thrust, and he may have been described as a Nazirite, but he was certainly not crucified. How a mystery-drama, based on a sacrifice and a meal of this order, became transformed into a narrative of the arrest, trial and execution of a prisoner by the Jewish and Roman authorities will pass the comprehension of any person of ordinary intelligence.

[1] L. G. Rylands, op. cit., p. 46.

If we follow the second clue—the occasional sacrifice of a king's son in time of crisis—we reach another result. The times were indeed critical enough in the days of the Herods to prompt such a revival. But if such a reversion to an ancient rite took place, it must have had a certain character. The victim must have been regarded as of royal descent, as belonging to the house of David. He must have been arrayed in royal robes, and he must have perished in them. The ceremony must have been august and dignified. If this was the character of the ancient rite as last performed, not a trace of it remains in the story of the crucifixion, which is essentially a death of ignominy and shame, unless indeed the title " King of the Jews " and the description of the victim as " Son of David " are to be attributed to the remembrance and continuance of the Phœnician myth and practice. Mr. Robertson struggled hard against this conclusion, which is the inevitable deduction from his own premises. Still clinging to the idea that in the last public sacrifice three malefactors perished, he thought it possible that " the sacrificers could by their ritual of mock-crowning and robing, distinguish one of the malefactors from his fellows: and by calling the others what they were, while he was paraded as king, they would attain the semblance of an august sacrifice."[1] I want to treat every suggestion of Mr. Robertson's with proper respect, but this seems to me flatly impossible. A child could see that not even the semblance of an august sacrifice could be obtained in this way.

[1] *Pagan Christs*, p. 182.

Mock-crowning and robing can be only the parody of such a ritual. They cannot possibly be the fulfilment of it or the substitute for it. It is plain that the high august rite of expiation and propitiation by the sacrifice of a king's son, cannot have been associated with the execution of three malefactors.

It is equally impossible to associate any form of crucifixion with this solemn sacrifice. Mr. Robertson tried to do so by frequent references to the account given by Dio Cassius of the death of Antigonus. "The historic crucifixion, scourging, and subsequent slaying of Antigonus, the last Asmonean King of the Jews, by Mark Antony, would further supply the motive for the story of Jesus having been crucified with a parade of the king title as Antigonus doubtless would be."[1] "The crucifixion of Antigonus would alone set up an enduring impression in Syria and Egypt."[2] In *Pagan Christs* (p. 181) Mr. Robertson went further. He suggested that the execution would recall acts of expiation and propitiation. "Such an act the Jews saw, as it were, performed for them when the Romans under Antony, at Herod's wish, scourged, crucified (lit. 'bound to a stake') and beheaded Antigonus, the last of the Asmonean priest-kings, in the year 37 B.C." The suggestion is that the idea of a crucified king as a sacrifice would thus be kept alive and may have been reduced to ritual form. Mr. Robertson noted that "Josephus does not give the detail of the crucifixion, and most of the Christian historians

[1] *Christianity and Mythology* (1st ed.), p. 396.
[2] Ibid., p. 402.

ignore it." Curiously enough, in none of his references did Mr. Robertson quote his original authority exactly, and he became increasingly blind to the real significance of the incident. Dio Cassius says, "He (Antony) scourged Antigonus, having bound him to a cross (or stake)— (an indignity) which no other king had suffered at the hands of the Romans—and after this he also slew him." The reference in Josephus consists of a quotation from Strabo. "Antony ordered Antigonus to be brought to Antioch and there to be beheaded: and this Antony seems to me to have been the very first man who beheaded a king. . . . He thought that this dishonourable death would diminish the value the Jews had for the memory of Antigonus." It is clear from Dio Cassius that Antigonus was not crucified. He was treated dishonourably and put to a dishonourable death, so that the Jews might cease to venerate his memory. It is obvious that no Jews can have seen an act of expiation as it were performed for them when the Romans beheaded Antigonus. What the story of Antigonus shows is that if Jesus was acclaimed as king of the Jews, he would have been put to death by the Romans, with all the marks of shame and ignominy recorded in the gospels. In other words, the evidence of Dio Cassius and Josephus confirms the belief that the gospels describe accurately a historic execution. In any case, of the august ritual, in which Kronos sacrificed Ieoud, not a vestige remains in the description of the death of Jesus in the gospels.

It is not surprising that in the long run

Mr. Robertson soft-pedalled Phœnicia and con-
centrated on Rhodes and the mock-king of the
Roman Saturnalia and Babylonian Sacaea. The
Palestinian rite was an annual sacrifice as in
Rhodes, not an emergency measure as in Phœnicia.
The victim personated " Jesus, the Son of the
Father," = Jesus Barabbas. In connection with a
Palestinian rite, a two-fold evolution may have
taken place. " At a certain stage, whether by
regal or other compulsion or by choice of the
devotees, the annual rite of sacrifice became a
mere ritual or mystery-drama—as in other cases
it became a masquerade. The former evolution
underlay the religions of Dionysus, Osiris, Adonis
and Attis: *the latter may or may not have gone
on alongside of the former.*" The former evolution one would naturally suppose must underlie
the Jesus-cult. Then the Palestinian rite as last
performed must have conformed to the Rhodian
type. In this case, the victim was a criminal condemned to death who was released to be sacrificed.
He was given wine to drink, and led outside the
city, where he was dispatched by having his throat
cut. In this form of sacrifice there is no sacrificial
meal and no cross. If this was the rite as last
publicly performed, the gospel narratives and the
drama on which they are based preserved only
a confused recollection of the facts that the victim
was a condemned criminal released to play the
part of Jesus Barabbas, and that he was given wine
to drink and was led out of the city. Nothing else
in the story has any connection with the solemn
rite of human sacrifice as last publicly performed.
The Supper, the Agony and Betrayal, the Denial,

the Two Trials, the crucifixion itself apart from two or three meagre details, the burial and resurrection, have no connection with the Palestinian rite. It is strange that a drama which was at bottom a perpetuation of the old Palestinian rite should turn out to have so little connection with the rite it was meant to perpetuate. The sacrificial foundation of the drama embodied in Matthew xxvi. 17–xxviii. 10 is slight and negligible: the superstructure is so elaborate as to hide it.

There is, however, another possibility, the public masquerade. After all, the *public* performance of an august solemn rite of human sacrifice in Palestine about 2,000 years ago is unlikely, and inconceivable at Jerusalem. Possibly in Galilee or Samaria, a group might secretly maintain such a rite. At an out-of-the-way place like Gilgal, such a rite might have been performed, and this suggestion of Gilgal is attractive because Gilgal is associated with Joshua, who is, as we shall see, a pre-Christian Jesus-God, and with a little ingenuity, Gilgal may be confused or rather identified with Golgotha. An actual rite of human sacrifice may have been privately performed in Gilgal. But even if no such practice persisted, the public masquerade might have gone on in Jerusalem, and an esoteric circle of devotees of the Jesus-cult would read deeper meanings into the masquerade itself. To the public, it would seem a parody and a jest: to the devotees, it would recall the rite that meant so much. If, then, they chose to embody their memories and their meanings in a mystery-drama, it would reflect, in disguise of course, many of the features of the public masquerade.

To be more explicit, the Jews may have had their equivalent of the Babylonian Sacaea or the Roman Saturnalia. In these festivals, a mock-king is appointed and does what he likes—during five days, in the case of the Sacaea. At the close of the feast, he is degraded and becomes the victim of a real or a mock-sacrifice. Philo has a story of a lunatic named Karabas being paraded as a mock-king, with mock-crown, sceptre and robe in Alexandria. This was done, he says, in ridicule of the Jewish King Agrippa, but it may point to a kind of Guy Fawkes celebration among the Jews. Karabas may be a mistake for Barabbas, and perhaps in connection with the feast of Purim, a criminal was released to reign as Mordecai for a few days, only to be hanged as high as Haman at the end. The victim in such a public masquerade may have been called " Jesus Barabbas," " Jesus, the Son of the Father." "What the gospel story *proves* is that it was known to have been a *practice,* either at Jerusalem or elsewhere, to release a prisoner to the multitude in connection with a popular festival, which might or might not have been the Passover. The release may have been for the purpose either of a religious masquerade or of a sacrifice. Either way, the religious rite involved was a rite of ' Jesus Barabbas '—Jesus the Son of the Father—and it involved either a real or a mock-sacrifice, in which the ' Son ' figured as a mock-king, with robe and crown."[1] It is a little difficult to have

[1] *The Jesus-Problem,* p. 38.

it both ways. If the prisoner was released for the purpose of a religious (?) masquerade, he cannot have been released for a sacrifice of the Rhodian type, and vice versa. But like Dionysus, Mr. Robertson could ride two asses simultaneously. The mystery-drama, apparently, in its original form, included features drawn from the religious masquerade and the rite of sacrifice. It is a strange business, for to those who created the mystery-drama, the Son of the Father was no mock-king. He was the only true king of Israel, or in terms of the ancient myth and ritual, he represented the true king's only son. All mockery is out of place, yet these devotees based their drama not on their genuine rite, but on the parody of it in a ritual like the Sacaea. The human sacrifice as the members of the Jesus-cult performed it, has disappeared behind a hateful parody. As Mr. Robertson was careful to point out, his case did not depend only on the parallels between the story of the crucifixion and the proceedings of the Sacaea and the Saturnalia. Still " the scourging, the royal robe, the mock-crown, were all part of those rituals, which thus conform in parody to the ritual of the mythic sacrifice of Ieoud, son of Kronos, probably parodied in the ritual for the victim sacrificed to Kronos at Rhodes."[1] As it happens, scourging does not figure in the ritual either in Phœnicia or Rhodes, but if the original drama was based not on the Palestinian rite, but on a parody of it, then the

[1] *The Jesus-Problem*, p. 52. According to this argument, the mystery-drama was based not on the original sacrifice itself, but on a parody of a parody of it. It must have resembled the soup of the soup of the hare in the Khoja's story.

scourging and the mockery as well as the release of a prisoner are all features of the rite as last publicly performed. Crucifixion as the mode of sacrifice and the inscription over the cross may also be original. But once again, the Supper, the Agony and Betrayal, the Denial, the Trials, the Burial and the Resurrection have no intimate connection with the ancient rite and the primitive mystery-drama.

By way of compensation, Mr. Robertson in *The Jesus-Problem*[1] announced a great discovery. The public masquerade holds the clue to the Triumphal Entry, the Cleansing of the Temple, and the change of attitude on the part of the crowd. The mock-king was deliriously welcomed at the beginning of the feast, and in the same way Jesus was acclaimed on his entry into Jerusalem. The vigorous exercise of authority in the temple courts is no longer strange. The mock-king was a privileged person and could do what he liked—for five days! At the end of the period, the crowd that welcomed him at the beginning of the feast turn and demand his execution. Here at last we come upon the original rite and can reconstruct the earliest form of the mystery-drama. In the first scene, in response to popular demand, the authorities, Jewish or Roman, release a prisoner to play the part of Jesus Barabbas in a festival like the Sacaea. The normal procedure was that the mock-king made a triumphal entry into the city riding on an ass or a couple of asses. So the second scene would depict this triumphal entry. Then for five days he acted as a king of misrule. This would be represented

[1] Op. cit., p. 42.

by a third scene, the Cleansing of the Temple courts. At the close, his death was demanded. Further scenes displayed the mockery and degradation, the scourging and the crucifixion. There is still no place in the earliest mystery-drama for the Supper, the Agony and Betrayal, the Denial, the Trials, the Burial, and the Resurrection.

If there is any truth in Mr. Robertson's two theses, that the closing narrative of Matthew is a drama and that the drama is based on some form of human sacrifice, the conclusion we have now reached seems the best, if not the only tenable one. For consider, if the mystery-drama was influenced at all by the parody, by the mock-sacrifice of the mock-king, it can only have been at the early stages of its development. As soon as the devotees of the Jesus-cult realized that people equated their Jesus with the Jesus Barabbas of the public masquerade, they inserted the express reference to Jesus Barabbas to make it clear that the Jesus whom they worshipped, the Jesus who was crucified, was *not* this object of popular ridicule. After that, no details from the Jewish equivalent of the Saturnalia could have been introduced into the play. All such details must belong to the earliest form of the mystery-drama. At least the scenes already named —release of a prisoner to be Jesus Barabbas, the Triumphal Entry, the mockery, the degradation, the scourging, the crucifixion—are primitive. As the rite as last performed may have been a hybrid rite, perhaps the Supper and the Resurrection in some form are equally primitive. Everything else is later. Certainly the Agony, the Betrayal, the Denial and the Trials must be later.

This is a strange and disconcerting conclusion. It is very difficult to believe that the devotees of the Jesus-cult could have borrowed so much from a parody which revolted them. But the facts inexorably point this way, it seems. And Mr. Robertson, we must assume, would never have advanced such a conclusion except under stern logical necessity, for it involved him in heavy sacrifices. Before he realized their true nature, he had traced the Triumphal Entry and the Cleansing of the Temple to two quite distinct and separate myth-motives.[1] The Triumphal Entry was suggested by the triumphant progress of Dionysus during which the god crossed a river mounted on two asses. This parallel was very convincing as it explained the two asses in Matthew's narrative, which narrative Mr. Robertson, in defiance of modern scholarship, normally regarded as the earliest. The Cleansing of the Temple is derived from a representation of Osiris armed with a whip. In the light of the new knowledge, these pretty fancies must be surrendered and two sections of *Christianity and Mythology* have become waste paper. But there is worse to follow.

By this development of his second thesis, Mr. Robertson completely undermined his first thesis. He claimed that the Last Supper, the Agony, the Betrayal, the Trials, the Crucifixion and the Resurrection were a coherent drama, and that the narrative which was a transcription of this drama was added to the Primitive Gospel. On this claim he confidently challenged criticism. But no critic need stir. Mr. Robertson shattered his own case.

[1] *Christianity and Mythology* (1st ed.), pp. 358 and 366 f.

He showed that the episodes in question do not form a coherent drama, and do not belong together, and that the crucifixion is inseparably bound up with the triumphal entry and the cleansing of the temple, being essential parts of the same ritual. The episodes which Mr. Robertson arbitrarily isolated were not scenes in a mystery-play, and were never added to a " Primitive Gospel." The development of thesis No. 2 undermined thesis No. 1, and the framer of the theses became the author of his own discomfiture.

For clearly when once he had decided that the real clue to the nature of the underlying ritual was to be found in the Barabbas incident, Mr. Robertson could no longer retain the Betrayal as part of the original drama. The Betrayal, sacrificially interpreted, corresponds to the practice of buying a victim with a price, and this is incompatible with the use of criminals and with the release of a prisoner to play the part of Jesus Barabbas. In his last book, *Jesus and Judas,* he wrote, " We are forced to note what the biographical school, down to Abbé Loisy and Dr. Joseph Klausner of Jerusalem, have so strangely failed to see, that the story of the betrayal is a documentary interpolation in the synoptics—an *addition* to a narrative in which originally *the betrayal did not figure.*"[1] It may be some consolation to Abbé Loisy and Dr. Klausner to learn that till the last moment Mr. Robertson failed to see it himself. One of the arguments to which Mr. Robertson attached most weight when seeking to demonstrate the dramatic character of Matthew xxvi. 17 to xxviii. 10 was the incongruity

[1] p. 25.

in ch. xxvi. 45, 46, where Jesus says, " Sleep on now and take your rest," and adds abruptly, " Rise, let us be going." This, we were assured, could only arise as an error in transcribing a play. In his last book Mr. Robertson upbraided Abbé Loisy for not seeing that verse 46 and following is a documentary interpolation in a narrative! The sections, Matthew xxvi. 21-25, and 46-60 and xxvii. 3-10, which are concerned with the Betrayal, were all added after the drama had been transcribed and reduced to narrative. The story of Peter's denial is a later addition, so at least xxvi. 33-35 and 69-75 must be classed with the Betrayal sections. These sections were freely drawn on as proofs of the dramatic origin of the whole narrative, and now it appears that they are not dramatic at all. They are interpolated additions to a previously existing narrative. So we now have Mr. Robertson's authority for rejecting the whole case he put forward in support of his first thesis. He still blamed critics for missing " the textual evidence which goes to prove that the five-act story of the Supper, the Agony, the Capture, the Crucifixion, and the Resurrection was a dramatic text, added to the gospels."[1] The textual evidence is easy to miss, since it is non-existent, but the internal evidence from literary characteristics, Mr. Robertson himself destroyed, when he decided to remove the Betrayal and Denial stories as interpolations, though he had previously insisted that they were essential parts of a coherent drama. And if they go, it is pretty clear

[1] *Jesus and Judas*, p. 70. It should be noted that in previous references *the Betrayal* is regularly mentioned as an integral feature of the five-act story. In his last book, Mr. Robertson silently substituted " the Capture."

that the story of the Agony cannot be retained, and if that is removed, the scene of the Capture is also doubtful. These doubts are confirmed by our reliance on the Barabbas incident. If in the rite as last performed the victim was a prisoner released to play the part of Jesus Barabbas, a drama based on such a rite had no room either for the Agony-scene or for the Capture. These also are late additions. The fact is, that of his first thesis Mr. Robertson left nothing standing.

With the destruction of his first thesis, the presupposition on which *Pagan Christs* is based simply disappears. If Jesus is to be a variant of the dying and rising God, it is absolutely essential that the story of his death and resurrection derive from a special source which stands by itself, quite disconnected from the Primitive Gospel. The development of Mr. Robertson's own argument shows that he was unable to maintain this position.

CHAPTER X

THE CRUCIFIXION: SACRIFICIAL RITE OR HISTORIC EXECUTION?

IT will by now be apparent that the attempt to find the origin of the story of the Cross in a rite of human sacrifice is perfectly hopeless. None of the details for which Mr. Robertson adduced sacrificial parallels would be regarded as sacrificial by any unprejudiced observer. Of the few details which show some distant resemblance to sacrificial usages, still fewer can have had any connection with the elusive Palestinian rite as it was last performed. In the greater part of the narrative—the Agony, the Capture, the Denial by Peter, the Trials, the Burial and Resurrection—Mr. Robertson himself could find no connection with any sacrificial rite. On his own confession, the Betrayal has no point of contact with the rite as last performed. The details for which Mr. Robertson with difficulty discovered sacrificial parallels are for the most part perfectly intelligible in a narrative of an actual execution. The scourging was a normal feature of a Roman crucifixion: it was not a regular feature of human sacrifice. The mockery and degradation by the soldiers is a probable occurrence in the execution of a prisoner condemned to death as king of the Jews. In spite of the assertions of many writers to the contrary, there is no discernible parallel between the mockery of Jesus by the soldiers and the treatment of the mock-king of the Carnival.[1] This episode cannot have originated in the usages of a festival like the Saturnalia, still less can it derive from an august sacrifice of a king's son. In the story of an execution, it is natural. In a ritual of human sacrifice it is unintelligible. For the offer of drugged wine to the condemned prisoner, we have the evidence of the Talmud that this was a charitable custom maintained by some of the wealthy women of Jerusalem. That the victims of human sacrifices were sometimes drugged with narcotics is true enough, but as a proof of Mr. Robertson's thesis, the fact has not the slightest importance. The dividing of the garments of the prisoner among the executioners is known to have been the custom among the Romans. We do not know that any such custom belongs to any rite of human sacrifice. Similarly, there is evidence from various quarters that in connection with crucifixion and impaling as punishments, the executioners gave or withheld a drink, as they wished to hasten or retard the death of the prisoner. The cry of Jesus, " I thirst," and the offer of wine by the soldiers is a perfectly credible incident in an execution.[2] We have no reason to think that it corresponds to any sacrificial ritual. The leg-breaking and the spear-thrust, which are found only in John, may be accidental rather than normal features of

[1] See Goguel, *La vie de Jésus*, p. 513.
[2] Cf. Goguel; op. cit., p. 527.

the punishment of crucifixion, though Lactantius describes the leg-breaking as the prevailing custom, and Origen says it was the usual practice of the Romans to stab under the armpits those who were crucified. Mr. Robertson asserted that the statement of Lactantius is without foundation,[1] but I am inclined to believe Lactantius for two reasons. Lactantius certainly knew more about crucifixions than Mr. Robertson did, and unlike Mr. Robertson, Lactantius had no axe to grind However, even if the incidents in John are unusual and even if they are unhistorical, the attempt to trace them back to usages in human sacrifice explains neither their origin nor their significance. The parallels from the Khonds and from Albania are completely irrelevant and possess no evidential value. There is no feature of the story of the crucifixion which is not readily intelligible and in place in a narrative of a Roman execution in Jerusalem in the time of Pilate. There is no feature which becomes more natural and more intelligible when regarded as a sacrificial usage, and most details become meaningless when we attempt so to regard them.

If we take a wider sweep and consider the episodes associated with Judas and Barabbas, it was clearly a mistake on Mr. Robertson's part to retain his sacrificial clue in the case of the Betrayal, when once he had decided that it was a late insertion, and an insertion not into the drama based on sacrifice, but into the narrative of an execution based on such a drama. What likelihood is there that into a narrative of an execution whose origin in a rite in which the victim was a criminal was no longer

[1] *Pagan Christs*, p. 121.

realized, anyone would insert an incident based on a still earlier usage, which was no longer in vogue when the rite was last performed? The suggestion of such an origin for the story of the Betrayal is as preposterous as it is unnecessary. If the Betrayal by Judas is unhistorical, it is a legend naturally associated with the execution of a Messianic claimant. There is no natural connection between betrayal and human sacrifice. Nor is there any valid reason why we should question the betrayal as an historic incident. That we imagine the arrest might have been effected without the intervention of Judas, and that we are in the dark as to his motive, are not adequate reasons for doubting the record. But whether history or legend, there is obviously no connection between the story of the Betrayal and the practice of purchasing a sacrificial victim with a price. It is passing strange that Mr. Robertson ever supposed there was.

As to the Barabbas-incident, its historicity has been questioned on the ground that we have no external evidence to corroborate the assertion that it was the custom of the procurator to release a prisoner whom the crowd selected at the Passover. If this absence of evidence is fatal to the narrative as it stands, it is equally fatal to Mr. Robertson's claim that it was the custom to release a prisoner to play the part of Jesus-Barabbas. This is refuted both by the lack of corroborating evidence and by the fact that there was no part of Jesus-Barabbas for anyone to play. There is no hint of a sacrificial ritual in the Barabbas-incident. And now we have some evidence from the papyri in support of the statement in the gospels. In the last edition of

Light from the Ancient East, Deissmann printed two documents which forbid us to dismiss the claim of the Barabbas-incident to be simple history. One of these, a Florentine papyrus of the year A.D. 85, supplies a very noteworthy parallel to Mark xv. 15. In the words of the evangelist, " And so Pilate, willing to content the people, released Barabbas unto them, and delivered Jesus, when he had scourged him, to be crucified."

The papyrus, containing a report of judicial proceedings, quotes these words of the governor of Egypt, G. Septimius Vegetus, before whom the case was tried, to a certain Philion: " Thou hadst been worthy of scourging . . . but I will give thee to the people."[1]

It is clear that Roman governors had the kind of power which Pilate exercised at the Passover. Our texts show that such a practice was recognized in Roman administration. The gospels afford no proof that any such release of a prisoner took place in Judaea in connection with a carnival-king.

It would be tedious and it is surely unnecessary to expose the irrelevance of sacrificial clues in the remaining instances, to point out for example that the triumphal entry and the cleansing of the temple courts have a clear and intelligible place in the course of historic events which led up to the arrest and execution of Jesus and have no connection with the treatment of a mock-king, or to stress the absurdity of trying to derive the whole conception and characteristic features of the public ministry of Jesus in the Primitive Gospel, which on Mr. Robertson's hypothesis had no doctrine of sacrificial

[1] See Deissmann, op. cit. (4th ed.), p. 269, n. 7.

death, from a sacrificial usage—the bribery of the victim with a year's licence—which again on Mr. Robertson's hypothesis had been long since abandoned and forgotten even by those elusive Jews who are supposed to have been still familiar with a human sacrifice in which the victim was a criminal.

Before we close our survey of this aspect of Mr. Robertson's second thesis, we may draw attention to two striking features of Mark's narrative which certainly suggest that he is offering us early and genuine reminiscence of an actual historic event. The first of these details Mr. Robertson did not attempt to explain as sacrificial in origin. The second he did try to include in his general theory, but the essay was ill-judged.

In Mark xv. 21 we read, "They forced Simon a Cyrenian who was passing on his way from the country (the father of Alexander and Rufus) to carry his cross."

This incident is the subject of a remarkable section in *Christianity and Mythology* (1st ed., pp. 368-9), where " the cross-bearing by Simon of Cyrene " is with some degree of probability traced to an artistic representation of a Pagan myth—to wit, the myth of Herakles setting up the two pillars at Gades.

In ancient art, he is actually represented carrying the two pillars in such a way under his arms that they form exactly a cross. Here, perhaps, we have the origin of the myth of Jesus carrying his own cross to the place of execution.

Then Mr. Robertson proceeds:

Singularly enough, the three synoptics substitute

for Jesus as cross-bearer one Simon, a man of Cyrene,
" coming from the country "—a way of suggesting,
perhaps, that he was strong. Cyrene is in Libya, the
legendary scene, as we saw, of the pillar-carrying
exploit of Herakles: and in Palestine Simon, Semo,
or Sem, was actually a God-name, representing the
ancient Sun-god Semesh. . . . What more likely than
that a representation of the Sun-Hero Simon . . .
carrying his pillars cross-wise, should come to figure
as that of a man Simon carrying a cross? The two
versions of the cross-bearing satisfy us that the story
is a myth: is any hypothesis more probable than that
Simon the Cyrenian's task is a variant of that of the
Cyrenian Simon-Herakles?

In the face of such paragraphs as these, it is difficult for anyone to claim any scientific value for
Mr. Robertson's speculations. Note the utter want
of critical principle. We have previously observed
that Mr. Robertson had no fixed ideas as to the
literary relations of his sources, yet normally he
regarded Matthew as the earliest gospel, and here
in forgetfulness of his own usual assumption and
in defiance of all critical study, he described the
three synoptics as correcting the incident in John,
substituting Simon for Jesus as the cross-bearer.
This is singular enough. When and why did Mr.
Robertson come to regard John as the earliest
gospel, and why did he never communicate his
reasons to the public? Then the existence of two
divergent versions of the incident satisfied Mr.
Robertson that the incident itself is a myth. He
was easily satisfied. No serious historian would
commit himself to a criterion so absurd. It is not
surprising that Mr. Robertson discovered myths
everywhere.

Look again at the parallel itself. In the picture referred to, Herakles carries one pillar under his right arm and the other over his left shoulder. As the first slopes up, and the latter slopes down, they appear to cross one another: but they certainly do not form exactly a cross, nor do they remotely resemble a cross. No one could have mistaken the two pillars for a cross, unless he were labouring under an obsession which led him to see crosses everywhere.

Mr. Robertson's accustomed courage in philology is also in evidence in this paragraph. Simon is a Greek name in use among Jews in the Hellenistic period. It means "Snub-nosed." It has no connection with Shem (="name" or "sign") and Shemesh (=the sun), the root of Samson (Shimshon). Mr. Robertson omitted the h, after the initial s, which is necessary for a fair transliteration, and so increased the resemblance to Simon. That is singular enough. But the important point is that the faith in a Sun-hero Simon lacks philological support.

Finally, how did Mark come to speak of this Simon as the father of Alexander and Rufus? Surely, Herakles must have had two sons with those names. Is the reference a late addition—Mark perhaps adding the detail to the three evangelists who must for the moment be held to have preceded him, or else some later copyist inserting the phrase in Mark?

Mr. Robertson took refuge in an interpolation-hypothesis. "If there be any rule made good by investigators of factitious narrative, it is that the later the version the more circumstantial are the details. In a story of which general scantiness of detail is the main characteristic, we have supererogatory information. If Mark were an early gospel and the names of Simon's sons were in it all along, how came it that they were not added in Matthew and Luke? The detail about Alexander and Rufus could have been interpolated by any copyist who supposed he could add a fact where facts were so few: and as Simon was one of the commonest of Eastern names, he had a wide field for conjecture."[1] It is interesting that the gospels are here assumed to belong to the class of factitious narratives—the point which Mr. Robertson had to prove. But the rule to which he appealed is of greater interest than the use of the question-begging epithet "factitious." It is well known that stories whether factitious or not, sometimes grow in circumstantial detail, but no one may claim that the more detailed the version of a given story, the later it must be. Had Mr. Robertson never heard of abridgment or of omission, and never met the ancient authorities who curtail their sources? Not only is the general rule unsound, but if literary study goes for anything, it has been shown to be inapplicable in the case of Matthew and Mark. Did Mr. Robertson regard Mark's version of the raising of Jairus' daughter as later than Matthew's because it is twice as long and much more detailed? The mere fact that Matthew and Luke are known to be compressing the information derived from

---

[1] *Christianity and Mythology*, p. 455. It was suicidal for Mr. Robertson to appeal to the principle, " the later the version, the more circumstantial the details." If he would not admit exceptions, he was bound in honesty to reject the reading, " Jesus Barabbas," in Matthew xxvii. 16, 17.

Mark or the equivalent record would suffice to warn us against assuming that the detail could not have been in the original edition of Mark because the other evangelists omit it.

There is no justification for regarding the detail as interpolated, but let us ask what did Mr. Robertson gain by such an hypothesis? Did it really help him? First of all, we may set aside the suggestion that a copyist would add a fact merely because facts were so few and details scanty. Certainly this particular interpolation would not be prompted by such a motive. *Such a reference to two living men could only have been made by a copyist who was writing for people who knew them.* It has no point otherwise. Moreover, it presupposes that Simon of Cyrene was known to the copyist and his readers as a historic person and that the events, real or supposed, took place when he could have taken part in them, i.e. within living memory. Incidentally we may observe that Matthew and Luke, writing for other circles, not interested in Alexander and Rufus, naturally omit the reference. But if this be not the explanation of their silence, if the interpolation-theory give a better explanation, the interpolation-theory itself requires a historic Simon of Cyrene with two sons, i.e. it requires all that we need to interpret the incident as history. It is noticeable that Mr. Robertson forgot Alexander and Rufus until Dr. Estlin Carpenter drew his attention to them, and his interpolation-theory was adopted as the easiest way of saving his main thesis, which was framed without considering all the facts. As often happens, the tempting way of escape from a diffi-

culty by means of an interpolation proves a blind
alley.

The other striking feature of Mark's story on
which I would like to dwell for a moment is the
cry of desolation, which Jesus is said to have
uttered in Aramaic or Hebrew. For this Mr.
Robertson offered an explanation which all his
admirers must regret. Here is his comment.
" Even the quotation put in the mouth of the dying
God-man, ' My God, My God, why hast thou for-
saken me?' has the effect of implying that he
had hitherto suffered voluntarily." Mr. Robertson
seems to have supposed that the series of expedients
adopted to secure the willingness of the victim
culminated in the subtle device of putting in the
mouth of the sufferer a literary quotation—a verse
from a Psalm—which might have suggested to a
highly educated and quick-witted audience, the
implication which only Mr. Robertson has ever
seen in it! If every other detail could be traced to
a sacrificial origin, this certainly cannot. Goguel's
judgment must stand. " The primitive Christian
consciousness could never have imagined the idea
of Jesus abandoned by God, and for Mark and
Matthew to express it, they must have felt bound
by the tradition." We may go further. Only in
a sincere and trustworthy tradition regarding a
historic happening could such a trait be found. A
narrative which refers to Simon as the father of
Alexander and Rufus and which reports this cry
of desolation is certainly early and as certainly
historic.

By this time it must be apparent that Mr.
Robertson's second thesis is improbable and irrele-

vant. Even so we have not exhausted the inherent difficulties of his whole view.

How, when and by whom did this sacrificial drama become mistaken for history? Do we owe the historical clothing to the dramatist or the evangelist? If the dramatist turned the thing into history, then he was not simply creating a substitute for a rite of human sacrifice. He must have had other ends and other motives. Consequently we have no reason to suppose that the drama was at bottom a perpetuation of a primitive rite. The *dramatist* would have no motive for sticking close to the primitive *rite*. But if the mistake was made by the evangelists, then Mr. Robertson was mistaken in regarding the evangelists as faithful transcribers of someone else's drama. He misrepresented them. If the earliest *evangelist* introduced Pilate and the historical colouring in general, he had no motive for sticking close to the primitive *drama*, and there is no reason to suppose he has done so.

How did a drama describing a sacrifice and written as a substitute for a sacrifice become mistaken for the history of an execution? Why was the primary motive, the guiding principle of the whole performance dropped out of the gospel-narrative? No doubt Mr. Robertson would have urged the view that all executions are *ipso facto* sacrifices. What about Saul's sons hanging before the Lord? What about " cursed by God is everyone that hangs on a tree? " Is not the death of Christ regarded as sacrificial throughout the New Testament? Let us grant that all executions could be regarded as sacrificial, and I grant it the more readily because it is fatal to Mr. Robertson's whole case. For since executions had a sacrificial aspect, this explains quite naturally how a genuine historic execution comes to present certain features in common with some forms of sacrifice, and also how a genuine historic execution would serve as the basis for a Christian doctrine of sacrifice. But when this is admitted, executions are still executions, and sacrifices are sacrifices. The primary aim of the execution is to punish the criminal, though the criminal may incidentally be held to be dedicated to God. The primary aim, at least, of the sacrifices at Rhodes, in Phœnicia, and among the Khonds, is to make an acceptable offering to a god. In the supposed drama embodying a sacrifice, this primary aim of placating a god or establishing communion with him must have been paramount. The whole judicial aspect must have been absent. How comes it, then, that the gospel-narratives are totally unaware of the sacrificial motive? How does a drama, based on sacrifice, give rise to a narrative of an execution, which ignores the sacrificial character of the events recorded? What possible motive was there for such a change, when the most important aspect of the event to the narrators themselves was still the sacrificial significance of the whole proceeding? How and why was a sacrifice transformed into a judicial execution?

Among the difficulties which Mr. Robertson detected in Frazer's theory is the following. The analogy with the Sacaea does not explain the subsequent status of the victim as Messiah. Curiously enough, neither does Mr. Robertson's theory explain this not unimportant point. How did a sacrificial victim representing a Saviour-God become identified or confused with the Messiah, who in the terms of the case must be a figure in history? This is part of a larger issue, which may be stated thus. How did a form of sacrifice which resembled that of the Khonds, and which consequently belonged to a low level of culture and could only, one would suppose, have been maintained by a group or groups of degraded Jews, who had lost sympathy with all that was best in their own religious traditions;—how did such a form of sacrifice become the womb and genesis of a faith which characteristically claimed to fulfil all that was best in the morality and religion of Judaism, and which regarded itself as the natural heir and supplanter of Judaism?

It would be easy to multiply such questions, and readers will search the literature of the Christ-myth in vain for answers to them. Mr. Robertson's hypothesis in particular accounts neither for the Cross nor for the Christ.

Here we must leave this most instructive study in inference. We have seen enough to know what Mr. Robertson meant when he said, "we may perhaps infer where we cannot trace the development that preceded the reduction of the Jesus myth to its present form." (p. 144.) Rationalists who infer where we cannot trace should not despise Christians who believe where we cannot prove. For inference means, apparently, flying in the face of existing evidence, adopting arbitrary judgments on literary questions to suit the convenience of particular arguments, supplying on presumption details which are perversely absent from the data, and clutching at any sort of straw —a bad text, an impossible meaning, a worthless bit of philology—providing only it lends colour to the hypothesis one wants to believe. None of these procedures are necessarily involved in believing where we cannot prove. They are apparently indispensable in inferring where we cannot trace.

CHAPTER XI

THE evidence adduced by Mr. Robertson for the practice of any form of human sacrifice among the Jews in Palestine 2,000 years ago is so scanty and unconvincing that it hardly deserves examination. At the best he only hoped to establish possibilities, and who can deny that among renegade or eccentric Jews some may have come into contact with queer primitive rites and have been willing to graft them on to their own religion? But when one asks what positive evidence there is for believing in the existence in the Mediterranean world and among the Jews of such a sacrament-sacrifice as is supposed to lie at the base of the mystery-drama, the answer is very simple: there is not a shred of evidence even from virulent anti-Semitic witnesses who would gladly have denounced such a sacrifice, had it existed among Jews. We may then be excused from discussing this aspect of the subject further and turn our attention to the search for a pre-Christian Jesus-God.

This last element in Mr. Robertson's second main thesis can be detached from its immediate context. Champions of the Christ-myth who reject the mystery-play and the sacrificial clues are persuaded that at least in regard to a pre-Christian Jesus-cult the author of *Pagan Christs* gave the right lead. On other issues the theorists are divided, on this they approach unanimity and repeat each other's arguments *ad nauseam*.

Jesus Barabbas plays a considerable part in the search for a pre-Christian Jesus. For it is generally assumed in Christ-myth circles that the original text of Matthew xxvii. 16, 17 gave the name of the prisoner whom Pilate released as Jesus Barabbas, and also that Jesus Barabbas is not a personal name but a ritual title. Many scholars, including Dr. Moffatt, accept this view of the text, but no unbiased student believes that Jesus Barabbas or Barabbas by itself can be regarded as a ritual title. The evidence from the Talmud is conclusive on this point, where Barabbas is frequently found as a personal name. The details are set forth in John Lightfoot, *Horæ Hebraicæ* (Works xi, p. 345). Professor T. W. Manson has drawn my attention to the note on the name Barabbas in Israel Abrahams' *Studies in Pharisaism and the Gospels* (second series, pp. 200, 201). Abrahams says, " The evidence for the use of Abba as a personal name is quite conclusive. . . . It may have been originally a title of honour (father, Master, Rabbi, cf. Abba Samuel) and thence become used as a proper name. But as Bacher points out, it may well be an abbreviation of Abraham." In either case the conjecture of the Christ-myth school is gratuitous and unsupported. There is no trace

I

anywhere of the use of Jesus Barabbas as a ritual title. References to Barabbas betray no sign of the cult-god whom we are seeking. The case must stand or fall with Joshua.

Was the successor of Moses, some sort of divinity? All believers in the Christ-myth are confident that Joshua of the book so named must have been an ancient deity. This fact, if it be a fact, does indeed give us a pre-Christian Jesus-cult, but it is of little interest until we establish its bearing on Christian origins. It might become significant if we could learn the character of Joshua as a god, and if it could be shown that the cult persisted into a late period. What do we know of this earlier Joshua-God? Mr. Robertson thought we might piece together some hints from the book of Joshua—a pseudo-history of late fabrication. Joshua, it seems, has some of the attributes of the Sun-God, was, in fact, a solar deity. The reference to the circumcision and the Passover in the book of Joshua, chapter v, suggests that his name was anciently associated with these ordinances. As Mr. Rylands puts it, " Joshua is said to have reinstituted—or, as would rather appear, instituted—the rite of circumcision, and would therefore in accordance with ancient mythological ideas have been regarded as the god of the rite."[1] The miracle of making the sun stand still is a greater prodigy than any attributed to Moses, and he must have ranked as high as Moses. " These things are not to be explained save on the view that he held divine status in the previous myth."[2]

[1] Op. cit., p. 38.
[2] *Pagan Christs*, p. 163.

130

A further discovery about Joshua may be made by what may be called the method of innuendo. He was probably "an Ephraimite deity," analogous to Joseph, whose legend has such close resemblance to the myth of "Tammuz-Adonis." This sentence drops the hint that Joshua, too, may be something of an Adonis. He figures as a possible variant of Tammuz a page or two later. But it is merely a hint: the argument is not explicitly drawn out. It would run as follows: Joseph is an Ephraimite god: Joshua is the same. Joseph resembles Adonis: therefore Joshua may have been like Adonis. The argument would be valid, if we had shown that all Ephraimite Gods were variants of Tammuz, or that Joshua and Joseph were alike in so many other things that they must be alike in this. As neither of these propositions is proved or probable, it is wiser merely to suggest that Joshua is the same as Adonis. Later on, the suggestion may be treated as a conclusion for which evidence has been offered!

Once started on his career, our Ephraimite deity rapidly attains high theological honours. In Exodus xxiii. 20-23, God promises to send an angel to go before Israel and bring the people into the place prepared for them. God's name is in or on the angel, and if the people obey him he will drive out from before them the Amorites and Hittites and Perizzites and Canaanites and Hivites and Jebusites. Now in Joshua xxiv. 11, the same list appears with the addition of the Girgashites, as representing the conquests effected by the Lord through Joshua. Must we not conclude, then, that Joshua is pseudo-historically identified with the promised angel?[1] Mr. Robertson confidently asserted that "non-theological minds will probably see some plausibility in an argument so borne out."[2]

The next stage in the argument must be carefully watched. Joshua was identified with the angel by some person or persons unknown, presumably when they noticed the parallel between Exodus xxiii and Joshua xxiv. But the angel "in virtue of his possession of the magical 'name' is in the Talmud identified with the mystic Metatron, who is in turn identifiable with the Logos."[3] We may here interpose that the mystic Metatron is by some derived from the Greek *meta thronon* = "behind the throne," and by others is supposed to be a corruption of Mithras. The more generally accepted view connects the name with the Latin, *Metator* = guide. Metatron belongs to the Roman period of Judaism. This mysterious power behind the throne is sometimes identified with Michael. However, the points established are that some readers of the books of Exodus and Joshua may have identified Joshua with the angel. Some Rabbinic authorities in the Talmud actually do identify the angel with the mystic Metatron which others again identify with the Logos. We are now ready for the amazing conclusion. "*Thus the name Joshua = Jesus is already in the (Hexateuch) associated with the conceptions of Logos,*

---

[1] *Pagan Christs*, p. 163.
[2] Ibid., p. 429.
[3] Ibid., p. 163.

Son of God and Messiah."[1]

It should be noted that Mr. Robertson just threw in the conceptions of Son of God and Messiah as a make-weight! But apart from that, the argument involves a number of curious assumptions for which no evidence is offered and for which no evidence is supposed to be necessary. It asks us to assume first that the Talmudic speculations concerning the Metatron and the angel of Jahweh, etc., are as old as the Hexateuch, and secondly that being as old they were well known to the writers of the Hexateuch. A critical reader will hardly swallow such absurdities, but no doubt believers in the Christ-myth will see some plausibility in an argument so borne out.[2]

If, however, you are not yet satisfied that in the Hexateuch Joshua was regarded as the promised angel and as the mystic Metatron, more evidence will be submitted to you. There is a Kabbalistic prayer attached to the Jewish liturgy for the New Year, which contains an obscure reference to Joshua as Prince of the presence, whatever that may mean. Then did not Mr. Hershon in his Talmudical commentary on Genesis draw attention to the fact that according to some Jews " the Week of the Son " (circumcision) was called the rite of " Jesus the Son "?[3] Great weight attaches to these items of evidence, for " neither Jewish nor Christian commentators latterly face the fact that in Jewish Talmudic

[1] *Pagan Christs*, p. 164. Mr. Robertson wrote " Pentateuch," but that is an obvious slip. He meant " Hexateuch."
[2] See Rylands, op. cit., p. 41.
[3] *Pagan Christs*, p. 166.

133

tradition there was a 'Jesus, the Prince of the Presence' and a rite of 'the Week of the Son' called by some 'the Week of Jesus the Son.'"[1] The first item confirms the identification of Joshua with the angel, and the second confirms the association of his name with circumcision.

We are not yet at the end of our resources. There is a remarkable Persian tradition which makes Joshua, the son of Miriam. Then in the Hexateuch Joshua was the son of Nun, and Nun means "fish," and a fish was an early Christian symbol. There must surely be something in this. Mr. Whittaker comes to our aid by arguing that in Jude, 5, "I will put you in remembrance how that *the Lord*, having saved the people out of the land of Egypt, afterward destroyed them that believed not," we must accept the variant reading "Jesus" as original and substitute it for "the Lord," and affirm without question that by "Jesus" is meant the Joshua of the Old Testament. It will follow from verse 6 that Joshua must have been conceived as a divine or supernatural being, since in verse 6 he judged fallen angels, and sitting in judgment on fallen angels was a function of the heavenly Messiah according to the book of Enoch.[2] The case for the pre-Christian Jesus may be rounded off by citing a passage from the Sibylline Oracles where the crucified Jesus of the Christians is confused with the Joshua of the Old Testament, and by recalling instances of the use of the name of Jesus in exorcism. Surely men would not have tried to

[1] *Jesus and Judas*, p. 207, cf. Rylands, p. 38.
[2] Rylands, op. cit., p. 41.

drive out demons in the name of a Jewish rabbi but only in the name of a divine being.

In this bewildering assortment of mountains constructed out of molehills, it is best to begin with the identification of Joshua with the angel. Mr. Robertson entertained some hope that the parallel between Exodus xxiii. and Joshua xxiv. would carry conviction to non-theological minds. Perhaps he despaired of theologians too soon, or perhaps the syllable "non" is a printers' error.

At least, it is interesting to find Mr. Robertson for once in cordial agreement with early Christian Fathers. Tertullian, for example, made the same identification of Joshua and the angel in arguing against the Jews. The grounds to which Tertullian appeals are somewhat different from and perhaps rather better than those on which Mr. Robertson relied. Yet both discussions belong to the same school of thought. Tertullian argues first that Christ's name is on the angel, and Joshua or Jesus is the name of the Christ, so clearly the angel must have been Joshua;[1] and second, John the Baptist is described as God's messenger (Angelum), and why should not Joshua have received the same title? In one respect Tertullian is vastly superior to Mr. Robertson. He did not suppose without a scrap of proof that the identification of Joshua with the angel was made *in the Hexateuch* or by the Jews or by the Samaritans. He recognizes that the identification rests on his own ingenious coupling of texts and

[1] With great wisdom, M. Couchoud in *Jésus, le Dieu fait homme*, p. 62, follows Tertullian and rests his case on the phrase, "My name is on him," which he holds applies both to the angel and to Joshua. M. Couchoud ignores Mr. Robertson's less effective argument.

phrases. Similar arguments appear in Justin Martyr and Origen.[1] The Christian Fathers identify Joshua with the angel and treat him as an embodiment of Christ, precisely because they have found the Christ in a Jesus who lived and died in the reign of Tiberius. For that reason, they take a fresh interest in his namesake in the Hexateuch. Apart from Christian speculation, the Joshua of the Old Testament was not associated with the angel or with the Logos or Messiah. The only doubtful exception is the late piece of Jewish angelology in the reference to Joshua, the Prince of the Presence. It is not even Talmudic, and it is worthless as evidence of any phase of pre-Christian thought. The passages in Jude and the Sibylline Oracles are definitely Christian and give no hint of a pre-Christian Jesus-God.

There is, of course, no justification for saying that Joshua was identified with the angel in the Hexateuch. As Mr. Robertson's argument implies, the identification was not made and could not have been made until the Hexateuch was complete and readers could compare Exodus and Joshua. It was never made except in Christian circles, moved by faith in the historic Jesus. In the Hexateuch, the Angel and Joshua are clearly distinct, since in Joshua v. 13-15, the angel appears to Joshua and announces that he has come as Captain of the Lord's host. The redactors of the Hexateuch knew nothing of Joshua's divine or angelic status. And as for the name Joshua being *already in the Hexateuch* associated with conceptions like Metatron

[1] For Origen, see Rylands, op. cit., p. 72.

and Logos and Messiah, the supposition is utterly ridiculous. When I pointed out to Mr. Robertson the absurdities involved in his argument, he charged me with childishly falsifying his assertions. However, when he restated his position in *The Jesus-Problem* (p. 83), he silently corrected his errors. He omitted the whole sentence which claimed that the name Joshua was *already in the Hexateuch* associated with conceptions like the Logos and the Messiah, and he did not repeat his reference to the Messiah. Instead he wrote, " The angel of the passage in Exodus is *in the Talmud* identified with the mystic Metatron, who corresponds generally with the Logos of Philo, the Sophia or Power of the Gnostics and the Nous of Plotinus." The correction does Mr. Robertson credit, but unfortunately it destroys his argument. If for the false assertion that the name of Joshua is in the Hexateuch associated with the Metatron and the Logos we substitute " the angel of the passage in Exodus is in the Talmud identified with Metatron," the argument simply disappears. The Talmud affords us no evidence of a pre-Christian identification of the angel with Metatron, and as for a pre-Christian Joshua with the status of a god or of an angel, it is completely silent. All this stuff about the angel and Metatron and the Logos in the Talmud is very interesting, but what has it to do with Joshua or even with pre-Christian Judaism? Precisely nothing. No one of the Talmudic authorities who identified the angel with Metatron ever identified Joshua with the angel. Neither in the Talmud nor in the Hexateuch is there the faintest trace of such an identification.

But surely some weight must be given to the passage in the Talmud where circumcision is described as "the week of Jesus the Son"? The passage does indeed deserve attention. It is in the Babylonian Talmud, Baba Bathra, fol. 60, col. 2, and the best and most recent edition renders it as follows: "A government has come into power which . . . does not allow us to enter into the 'week of the Son' (according to another version, 'the salvation of the Son')." In a footnote the Hebrew expressions are given and two alternative forms of the second, to wit, "the redemption of the Son" (Rashi) and "birth of a Son" (R. Tam). It is supposed that in times after Hadrian it was safer to refer to circumcision as "the week of the Son" or as "the salvation of the Son" than to mention it openly. In any case, Mr. Robertson was misled by Hershon, a converted Jew who found references to Jesus in the Talmud where they did not exist. No Jew ever called circumcision, the rite or "the week of Jesus the Son," and there is no sign in the Talmud of any close association of the name Jesus with the rite of circumcision.

It is hardly worth while to turn over this farrago of mares' nests any further. The arguments are worthless, but it is now time to ask, on what principle was this account of the pre-Christian Joshua constructed? Do Mr. Robertson and his followers start from a literary analysis of this pseudo-history? Are there, for example, literary grounds for assigning to the earliest Ephraimite strata the reference to the Passover and circumcision, which have usually been regarded as belonging to the later elements of the book? Is it clear that Joshua v. 13-17 is later than Joshua xxiv? If any definite theory of the composition of the book does determine this account of the god, it is very successfully concealed. It is equally impossible to detect any method of anthropological research behind this apparently haphazard collection of traits for Joshua.

If Mr. Robertson was the happy possessor of a scientific method by which the features of an original deity can be disengaged from the later picture of the human hero, he gave no hint as to the nature of this method in his account of Joshua. Nevertheless, his selection of attributes for Joshua was not merely fortuitous. Whether Mr. Robertson was conscious of it or not, the motive that guided him is perfectly transparent. He selected from the book of Joshua those items which helped him to imagine an Ephraimite deity like unto the Christian Jesus. Do the Christians place Jesus above Moses? Then the Ephraimite Joshua must have had a divine status equal if not superior to that of Moses. Is the Christian Jesus associated with the Passover? Then the Ephraimite Joshua must have been closely associated with the Passover. Did the Christian Jesus reinstitute or, as would rather appear, institute the rite of baptism? Then Joshua must have reinstituted or, as would rather appear, instituted circumcision. Was baptism in the name of Jesus? Then circumcision must have been the rite of Joshua the son. Is Jesus judge of men and angels? Then Jude must have regarded Joshua in the same light. Was Jesus regarded as the Logos? Then already in the Hexateuch Joshua must have been so regarded. Did Jesus die and rise again?

Then the Ephraimite deity, Joshua, must have resembled Adonis. (See Note I below.)

The motive guiding these baseless conjectures is quite simple, and once detected it robs the arguments, by which they are supported, of any scientific value. If Joshua were originally a deity—and he may have been—no one knows anything about him. Mr. Robertson and his followers can give us a portrait of this pre-Christian God, not because they know anything about him, but because they know what they want to know about him. That the Ephraimite Jesus-God is singularly like the Christian Jesus is not surprising: for he only exists as the latter's shadow. This account of Joshua as a divinity is just a fancy-portrait painted by prejudice.

NOTE I

In his anxiety to connect the pre-Christian Jesus with a sacrificial ritual, Mr. Robertson turned to the story of Abraham and Isaac for assistance. "The Syrian form of the name, Jeschu, closely resembles the Hebrew name Yishak, which we read Isaac, and that Isaac was in earlier myth sacrificed by his father is a fair assumption. We have here the inferrable norm of an ancient God-sacrifice, Abraham's original Godhead being tolerably certain, like that of Israel."

The weakness of the linguistic argument is sufficiently exposed in the following comment which I owe to Dr. Rendel Harris. "For the identification of Isaac (Yitzchak) and Joshua (Yehoshua), Mr. Robertson should have adduced some parallels. It is true that if we take the English spelling of Isaac and the

Arabic spelling of Jesus, we do obtain some similarity.
In the Hebrew, however, the two names do not agree,
either in consonants or vowels, except as regards the
initial letter. The proper parallel to be quoted would
be Romeo and Rosemary, or better still, Monmouth
and Macedon." No philology, however elastic, will
enable us to merge " Jesus, the son of the Father," in
" Isaac, the son of Abraham." Mr. Robertson would
have appreciated the Shakespearian allusion, however
reluctant he would have been to admit its devastating
effect on his argument.

NOTE II

To avoid overloading this chapter, I have refrained
from discussing Mr. Robertson's appeal to the *Apoca-
lypse of St. John* and *The Teaching of the Twelve
Apostles*, as affording evidence of a pre-Christian Jesus-
God. That both documents embody some pre-Christian Jewish material is probably true, but to derive
the references to Jesus from such material is sheer
perversity.

CHAPTER XII

SOME RATIONALIST PREJUDICES

WE have now contemplated rationally Mr. Robertson's hypothesis, and we have found that he himself has demolished his own original thesis of a mystery-drama and that the story of the crucifixion has no connection either with a rite of human sacrifice with many variants or with a pre-Christian Jesus-God. Such an examination should suffice to discredit the Christ-myth, but criticizing the Christ-myth is not unlike punching a feather-bed. Wherever you press it, it gives way, but it swells up in some other direction. If the advocates of the theory deign to notice my argument and admit the strength of it, they will at once say, Why did you not discuss something else? Robertson, after all, was only a pioneer. His first tentative theories naturally break down and few exponents of the Christ-myth support them any longer. The real strength of the case depends on W. B. Smith's investigations into pre-Christian Gnosticism or on Couchoud's studies in apocalyptic. Raaschke's thesis that Mark rather than an abbreviated version of Luke was Marcion's original gospel, or Couchoud's variant of it to the effect that the first gospel was the work of Marcion and that both Mark and Luke are editions of Marcion's original, would have attracted the attention of a serious critic. Alfaric's view of Mark as a creative artist who fashioned all his stories himself out of material drawn from the Old Testament and Paul, or Drews' idea that Mark's story is based on themes derived from star-maps and astral myths, would have been worth discussing. Or again the theories of Van Manen regarding Paul's epistles—theories so admirably expounded by Mr. Whittaker and so strangely elaborated by Mr. Rylands—might have been handled by a conscientious opponent. How like an orthodox scholar to take up Mr. Robertson's theses which never commanded wholehearted support and are now admittedly outmoded!

If an attempt is made to blunt the edge of criticism in this way it may be worth while to point out that the theories to which attention is invited are at least as irrational as the two theses we have analysed, and that all these theories involve the same untenable presuppositions and the same indefensible prejudices. If we had examined in detail Drews' astral-mythological theory, which treats Jesus, like Joshua of the Old Testament as a sun-god, and finds Aquarius, the man with the watering-pot, in John the Baptist, while Salome is identified with Andromeda and Pilate with I forget what, we could have made Mr. Robertson's theories seem like sheer common sense in comparison. The same result would have followed had we examined the strange reasoning whereby Mr. Rylands convinces himself that Romans i.–viii. consists of three separate documents from three separate hands, the first two chapters being written by a man who

believed in salvation by works, chapters iii.–v. by
one who held to justification by faith, while
chapters vi.–viii. come from one who believed in
salvation through mystical union with Christ.[1] If
J. M. Robertson cannot be saved, where will Arthur
Drews and L. G. Rylands appear? In my judgment
apart from the writings of J. M. Robertson, the only
contribution to the literature of the Christ-myth
worth closer consideration is the latest book by
P. L. Couchoud, *Jésus le Dieu fait homme* (1935).
Here at last is a fresh, vital and readable book.
Indeed it is the only volume on the Christ-myth that
can be read with genuine pleasure. The other
writings are for the most part heavy and wearisome
to a degree. The main reason why Dr. Couchoud's
book is alive is that he believes in Paul and Marcion
as persons and has definite conceptions of their
characters. Other Christ-myth theorists are as
hazy about Paul as they are about Jesus. If Dr.
Couchoud had had a vivid conception of Jesus as
a personality, he would have written not merely
an interesting but also a good book. But from the
standpoint of the historian, all writers of this
school, including Dr. Couchoud, are in the same
condemnation with Mr. Robertson. All of them
claim scientific authority for presuppositions and
prejudices which have no place in historical
criticism, and none of them handle evidence fairly.

All Christ-myth theorists start from a view of
the gospels as discredited witnesses—a view which
no scientific historian can accept and which rests
on rationalist prejudice and sheer ignorance. A
typical statement of this common characteristic

[1] *Did Jesus Ever Live?*, pp. 21, 22.

may be found in Mr. Whittaker's book, *The Origins of Christianity*, p. 21.

"Now the Gospels, to which the primary appeal has to be made, cannot be regarded as historical documents. They are of unknown authorship and of composite origin. Their probable date is more than two generations after the events they professedly record, and they are of miracle-stories all compact. The teacher never appears as a mere human being, but as 'the Lord,' the 'Son of God.' His birth is miraculous. His death on the cross is not described with accompaniments that were those of a Roman execution, but with the characteristic details of various rites of human sacrifice known in all parts of the world from India to Mexico. To all of them a mystic significance is attributed. As a teacher, he from the first claims authority to reverse the decisions of the ancient lawgivers of his nation: if he approves of the law, that, too, is by his authority. We are remote enough here from memoirs of some-one who really lived."

Let us look at these statements one by one, holding up to the last the suggestion that the gospels "are of miracle-stories all compact." The first reason for refusing to regard the gospels as historical documents is that "they are of unknown authorship." The statement is not strictly true, since there is no convincing reason against accepting the traditions which associate the names of Mark and Luke with the second and third gospels respectively. But even if it be true, since when have historians decided to treat anonymous documents as of no evidential value?

The next reason advanced in support of Mr. Whittaker's irrational thesis is that the gospels are of composite origin. This is true, and the fact discounts the force of the next consideration that "their probable date is more than two generations after the events they professedly record." For if the gospels are of composite origin, it means that they embody traditions which had been in existence long before the gospels themselves were written. So far from their composite origin leading the scientific historian to reject the evidence of the gospels, it tends to inspire confidence in it. For it is precisely this feature of the gospels which disposes, once and for all, of theories like that of Bruno Bauer, who "regarded Mark not only as the first narrator, but even as the creator of the gospel history, thus making the latter a fiction and Christianity the invention of a single original artist." The speculations of Drews and Alfaric regarding Mark are as out of touch with the known facts concerning the composite character and origin of the gospels as was the theory of Bruno Bauer. Mark's narrative is not a work of creative imagination. It is built up out of traditions which had taken shape long before the evangelist set out to tell the story. The old oral hypothesis which Mr. Robertson favoured, and the work of Form-critics since the war alike confirm us in the belief that the gospels are the outcome of a process in which traditions based on the memories of the first apostles were selected and moulded by the needs of the early Christian communities. The material in the Synoptic gospels is not affected for the most part by the events of

A.D. 70. It has taken shape in the experience of
the first generations of Christians, before the fall
of Jerusalem. The order in which the stories
about Jesus are narrated in the gospels is obviously
in large measure artificial, and it varies from one
gospel to another. The school of Drews ignores
this fact. Dibelius well brings out the bearing of
form-criticism (i.e. the critical account of the
formation of the gospel tradition) on Christ-myth
theories in the following paragraph. Drews views
the totality of the recorded life of Jesus " as a
myth, as a repeated passage of the sun through
the zodiac, or something like that. If the life of
Jesus had first been conceived as a myth and
had gradually been transformed into history, the
essential element in such a presentation would
have been the sequence of the several events.
Only from their succession could the mythical
interconnection result. We have seen, on the
contrary, that the sequence of the separate
(sections) is wholly unessential in the account
of the ministry of Jesus. The several Evangelists
have changed the sequence at their discretion.
Such accounts as have been preserved of the life
of Jesus, apart from the story of the Passion, were
detached pictures, to be used in preaching as
desired, always related to faith, but quite unlike that appearance of entirety that characterizes
a myth. Thus the method of form-criticism
enables us to recognize that the beginnings of
the story of Jesus are not embedded in myth, but
have their foundation in actual events."[1] Mr.
Whittaker is right. The gospels are of composite

[1] Dibelius, *Gospel Criticism and Christology*, pp. 71, 72.

147

origin. That gives the death-blow to the Christ-
myth, since it shows that the gospels must be
regarded as historical documents.

"The teacher never appears as a mere human
being, but as 'the Lord,' the 'Son of God.'"
What exactly is the force of this observation?
That the gospels were written by believers to
promote faith in Jesus as the Lord and as the
Son of God, i.e. as the Christ, is beyond dispute.
Is it on this account that we cannot regard them
as historical documents? If this is what is meant,
it is a very poor unconvincing argument. If men
came to believe, as they did, that they had found
in a Jewish rabbi or prophet the Messiah, the
Son of God, how could they better commend their
faith than by recording the actual sayings and
deeds of Jesus which had been the source of
their own conviction? That the gospels are pro-
pagandist documents based on preaching does not
in the least discredit them as historical witnesses.
Beyond a doubt Mark believed in Jesus as Christ
and Lord. This fact makes it the more interesting that with one possible exception in xi. 3,
the religious expression "the Lord" as descriptive
of Jesus occurs nowhere in Mark's narrative.
This, the language of Christian devotion, does
occur in the late spurious ending added to Mark.
It is also found thirteen or fourteen times in
Luke's gospel. The term, "Lord," in the vocative
addressed to Jesus occurs at most three times in
Mark. It is used much more frequently in
Matthew and Luke, and though it is not certain
that it is always used in the full religious sense,
it is evidence of the growing influence of

devotional usage on the form of the narrative.
In several instances, Matthew has "Lord," where
Mark has "teacher" or "rabbi." In all the
gospels, however, the words "teacher" or
"master" and "rabbi" are in constant use as
descriptive of Jesus, so much so that it is plausible to argue that in the earliest tradition Jesus
appeared primarily as teacher and prophet and
not as Lord and Christ. However that may be,
it is important to note that Mark, who believed
Jesus to be the Lord and Son of God, probably
never referred to Jesus as "the Lord" in his
narrative and very sparingly uses "Lord" as a
form of address directed to Jesus. The use of
the term "Son of God" is also curiously
restricted. It is clearly Messianic, and it has
not the associations of the Logos-doctrine as
Mark employs it. If Jesus is not a mere human
being, it is certainly in a human being that
Mark discovers the Son of God. The only
possible conclusion from the fact to which Mr.
Whittaker so happily draws our attention is the
trustworthiness of the tradition on which the
gospels are based. Even in such a matter as
the use of the terms "the Lord" and the "Son
of God," the tradition as we have it in Mark has
not been fully moulded to the form of the faith
to which it bears witness. Moreover, the contrast between Mark at this point and Matthew
and Luke, and still more the contrast between
Mark and John, show that a famous assertion
of W. B. Smith is the exact reverse of the truth.
W. B. Smith asserted, with J. M. Robertson's
approval, that "the received notion that in the

early Marcan narratives the Jesus is distinctly human and that the process of deification is fulfilled in John, is precisely the reverse of the truth. In Mark there is really no man at all: the Jesus is God, or at least essentially divine, throughout. He wears only a transparent garment of flesh. Mark historizes only. Matthew also historizes and faintly humanizes. Luke more strongly humanizes: while John not only humanizes, but begins to sentimentalize." The facts just adduced regarding the use of the expression, "the Lord," would of themselves bring to light the transparent absurdity of this assertion. The attentive reader of the gospels will have no difficulty in seeing that the received notion is strictly true and the attempt to reverse it a wilful travesty of the facts of the case. It is Mark who speaks with amazing freedom of the emotions of Jesus, of his anger and indignation, of his surprise and perplexity, of his grief and sorrow, of his compassion and love. It is Mark also who speaks of the sighs of Jesus, of his intensive or comprehensive gaze, and also of the gesture whereby he impulsively took children in his arms and fondled them. It is Mark who depicts Jesus as delighted with the wit of the Syro-Phœnician woman, as attracted by the sincerity of the rich young ruler, as so interested in the lawyer who answered discreetly, that he praised him. It is Mark who represents Jesus as asking questions for information and who reflects the freedom with which his disciples on occasion remonstrated with their Master. It is Mark who uses expressions which suggest that Jesus was limited in power, in knowledge and even in goodness. There is not a trace in Mark of Docetism, i.e. of the absurd idea that Jesus was a divine being wearing a transparent garment of flesh. Throughout, the Jesus of Mark is intensely and unmistakably human. Some of the features of his narrative to which we have alluded are preserved in the later gospels, but much is lost and more is modified. The later gospels become more decorous, more reverent in a conventional sense and more definitely theological. There is no excuse, and certainly no justification for W. B. Smith's preposterous assertion. Yet if this assertion is not true, the whole case for the Christ-myth goes by the board.

"His birth is miraculous." Undeniably in Matthew and Luke we have accounts of the birth of Jesus which the unbiased historian would probably treat as legendary. But what conclusions are we to draw from this fact? Speusippus, Plato's nephew, who succeeded his uncle as head of the Academy, apparently believed that the birth of Plato was miraculous. Must we therefore deny the existence of Plato or even assume that Speusippus was a dishonest liar whose evidence is not to be trusted on any point regarding Plato's life and teaching? Only a fool would draw such a conclusion. The presence of legendary accounts of the birth of Jesus does not even discredit Matthew and Luke as witnesses, and if the presence of such stories is held to weaken our confidence in the first and third evangelists, in all fairness the absence of any such story from Mark should enhance the value we attach to his earlier narrative. No doubt the idea of birth from a virgin-mother is associated with some mythical personages, but it is also associated with historic personalities and never with insignificant historic personalities. Whatever we make of them, whether they be legend or history or legend-and-history, the stories of the miraculous birth of Jesus imply at once his historicity and the greatness of the impression he made on those who knew him and believed in him.

"His death on the cross is not described with accompaniments that were those of a Roman execution, but with the characteristic details of various rites of human sacrifice known in all parts of the world from India to Mexico." Our careful examination of Mr. Robertson's theses entitles us to say that there is not the shadow of truth in this assertion, and we need not labour the matter further.

"To all of them (i.e. all the details), a mystic significance is attributed." Drews, W. B. Smith, and Mr. Rylands go further and say that every detail in Mark has a symbolic meaning. Even if the assumption were true, it would not justify us in treating as unhistorical the details in which the early Christians found mystic significance. Mr. Rylands naïvely states his critical principle in the following terms: "The scientific investigator will recognize here a confirmation of his working hypothesis that the Gospel as a whole is symbolism and will not accept anything in it as literally true, whether possible or not, until he has satisfied himself that it cannot be interpreted symbolically."[1] It would be strange if there is any historical incident, inside or outside the gospels, which cannot be interpreted symbolically. The working hypothesis that the gospel as a whole is symbolism, has nothing to do with scientific investigation, and to refuse to accept as literally true anything for which you can suggest a symbolical interpretation is merely an irrational prejudice which will preclude its victim from any chance of arriving at the truth regarding Christianity or any other historical phenomenon. From the fact that the details of the gospel-stories have been interpreted symbolically and may have had mystic significance for the Evangelists themselves, no scientific historian will conclude that the gospels are not to be regarded as historical documents.

Mr. Whittaker's last point I cannot understand at all. How the fact that Jesus taught with authority and reversed decisions of Moses, shows that we are remote enough from memoirs of someone who really lived, I simply cannot comprehend. It is just conceivable that a teaching of such sovereign freedom, had it occurred to some advanced individual, might have been presented under cover of some great name from the past as in the great pseudepigraphical[2] writings. It might have been attributed to Enoch or Isaiah or even to Joshua. If any group in Judaism had arrived at such an attitude they would never have been so silly as to attribute it to a fictitious character supposed to have lived in the reign of

[1] *The Evolution of Christianity*, p. 192.
[2] i.e. published under a false name.

Tiberius. The fiction would have been at once exposed. *It is precisely the freedom with which Jesus handles the Law that will convince the scientific investigator that in the gospels we have the memoirs of someone who really lived.*

I have left till last the statement that the gospels are of miracle-stories all compact. This is the real foundation of rationalist scepticism regarding the gospels as historical documents, and it is high time that it was recognized for what it is—an antiquated and exploded superstition. For writers of the Christ-myth it is axiomatic that miracles do not happen. Stories of the supernatural are, *ipso facto,* incredible and unhistorical. Documents which contain such stories are thereby shown to be worthless. Mr. Robertson assured us that, " *historically,* the supernaturalist narrative of the gospels has no authority for critical science."[1] He took for granted that all liberal thinkers, all enlightened persons, agree in discarding miracles as mythical. He treated all the miracles in the gospels as standing on the same dead level of incredibility. It does not matter that these stories differ both in character and attestation. Mr. Robertson insisted on a clean sweep, and never dreamed that a scientific historian would have any hesitation about it. Since the Liberals have surrendered the miraculous element, they must go further. The supernaturalist flavour is in the teaching as well as in the miracles. The story of the Cross is " stamped with supernaturalism in every sentence."[2] There may be some historical allusions in it. There

[1] *Pagan Christs,* p. 194 n.
[2] Ibid., p. 147.

may be, for example, some allusion to a story
" fortuitously preserved in the Talmud, that one
Jesus ben Pandira was stoned and hanged at
Lydda."[1] " The evidence is obscure, but even
such evidence gives better ground for a historical
assumption than the supernaturalist narrative of
the gospels."[2] Again, the testimony of Josephus
is assumed to be much more valuable than the
evidence of the gospels, because " one item of non-
supernatural historical testimony outweighs any
amount of supernaturalist record."[3]

Mr. Robertson and Mr. Whittaker agree in the
assumption that the presence of the miraculous
element absolutely discredits the gospels as
historical records. They would endorse Robert
Blatchford's sentence, " The fact that the gospels
teem with miracles destroys the claim of the
gospels to serious consideration as historic
evidence."[4]

Before we examine this presupposition in itself,
we may note that the scales are unfairly weighted
against the gospels. To put the gospel-narratives
on the one side as supernaturalist and the Talmud
and Josephus on the other as non-supernaturalist
is, to say the least, a rather naïve procedure. It
is a little surprising in rationalist critics who have
set out to demolish the attempt to put Biblical
literature in a class by itself. The division of
Christian versus Jewish and profane history cannot
be thus equated with the pseudo-division, supernaturalist and non-supernaturalist. Very little

[1] *Pagan Christs*, p. 194.
[2] Ibid.
[3] *Christianity and Mythology*, p. 455.
[4] *God and My Neighbour*, p. 100.

ancient testimony is entirely free from the supposed taint of supernaturalism, and least of all can the Talmud and Josephus be contrasted with the gospels in this respect.

The same irrational disparagement of the gospels as compared with the Talmud is incidentally revealed in the reference to the story of Jesus ben Pandira as *fortuitously* preserved. Apparently nothing in the gospels is fortuitously preserved. There everything is tendential and biased. But the Talmud and Josephus are just impartial records, it seems, and Mr. Robertson accepted as fortuitously preserved a story which is with reason believed to be inspired in the Talmud by anti-Christian prejudice. Jesus ben Pandira is most probably a mythical creation intended to disparage the story of the virgin-birth of Christ. There is no reason to believe the gospels to be more tendential than the Talmud or Josephus.

The general presupposition, however, is itself untenable. If we recognize that the gospels teem with miracles, does it follow that they have no value for critical science? No historical student who knows his business can endorse such a conclusion. Especially in religious history and in the history of mediæval Europe, we have constantly to use documents which are steeped in supernaturalism, and no one dreams of denying authority to them, whatever the personal belief of the inquirer may be as to miracles. Can the historian make no use of works like the dialogues of Gregory the Great or his letters concerning St. Benedict or the *Vita Antonii*, or Adamnan's life of St. Columba, written in three books, one of visions, a second of miracles, a third of prophecies, or the legendary *Little Flowers of St. Francis*? Do incurably supernaturalist narratives never give us any trustworthy and valuable information as to the character and influence of historic personalities? Genuinely scientific historians who totally disbelieve in miracles would never admit that supernaturalist narratives, whether in the gospels or out of them, have no authority for critical science.

I doubt if many students of Christian origins would now say with Matthew Arnold, "there is nothing one would more desire for a person or document one greatly values than to make them independent of miracles."[1] At least, it is clear that if the gospels did not contain miracles, if they gave us simply a moral teacher or a liberal theologian, they would be suspect as not emanating from the primitive group of humble folk with which Christianity claims to have originated. Those who are not ashamed of the democratic character of early Christianity will not regret that in their very supernaturalism they carry the hall-mark of a genuine popular tradition.

Beyond all this, we have to reckon with well-authenticated stories of miraculous healing which are more or less parallel to many of the miracles in the gospels. What we know of the power of faith in actual experience entitles us to say that, given the great personality, story after story in the gospels is unquestionable history. Mr. Robertson himself recognized the breakdown of all attempts to explain the miracle-stories as symbols and not as actual occurrences. " It can hardly be doubted that the

[1] Blatchford, op. cit., p. 100.

stories of healing made their appeal as simple miracles."[1] The stories were offered and accepted as accounts of actual occurrences, and in many instances their *bona fides* cannot be questioned on the ground that miracles do not happen, since similar miracles happened then and have happened since.

Plainly enough, on the whole question of the historical worth of supernaturalist narratives, writers of the Christ-myth school are completely fogged by the traditions of the older Rationalism which have long since been discarded by critical science. The axiom, Miracles do not happen, is quite useless for the purpose of historical inquiry. It does not allow you to rule out as *a priori* impossible a single miraculous story in the gospels. Nor does supernaturalism discredit a document as a historical authority. No open-minded thinker will now reaffirm this dogmatic rejection of the miraculous. The world of thought in which Christ-myth theorists move and have their being is dead beyond recovery. And this scientifically worthless presupposition regarding the supernatural is fundamental to their whole outlook. Without it they would never have begun their inquiries, and without it none of their results can stand.

[1] *The Jesus-Problem*, p. 208.

CHAPTER XIII

DOES THE CHRISTIAN FAITH NEED A HISTORIC CHRIST?

I HAVE charged the writers of the Christ-myth school with being incompetent critics, unable to handle evidence fairly. They ignore and transgress some of the more elementary standards of historical inquiry. For on what principles does a genuinely scientific historian proceed about his task? He will certainly not treat mere conjectures as historical fact. He will not lightly assume that all the statements in his texts which make against his own view must be interpolations. He will not rely incautiously on arguments from silence. He will not browbeat his witnesses, by insisting that they mean the reverse of what they say, or by refusing to make allowance for the margin of inaccuracy and inconsistency that is natural in all human testimony and particularly in a popular tradition. He will not insist that all apparent discrepancies must be real insoluble contradictions, nor will he assume that contradictory impressions and reports, conflicts of evidence, prove all the witnesses to be liars and prevent us from reaching any probable con-

clusions regarding the events and persons concerned. He will not seek to solve historical questions by appeals to theological prejudice, nor will
he confuse historical and theological issues. Judged
by these standards, no writer of the Christ-myth
school can be regarded as a genuinely scientific
inquirer in the field of history. It would be easy
to fill a whole volume with additional specific
illustrations of the sins of these writers against the
canons of historical criticism. But the evidence
provided by our previous investigations must suffice
for the present. We have yet to discuss more vital
matters.

What difference would it make to Christian
faith if Jesus could be shown to be a myth? This
is the most significant issue raised by the controversy over the Christ-myth. Until we have laid the
ghost of the groundless suspicion which condemns
the gospel-tradition as a whole, we shall not make
much progress with the work of distinguishing
history from interpretation in the gospels. But
even though we are convinced that the historicity
of Jesus is not now, and is never likely to be, open
to serious doubt, the inquiry into the religious
significance of his existence in the past remains of
interest. For the difference of current views concerning religion in general and Christianity in particular, are revealed very surely by the varying
degrees of importance which men attach to historic
happenings.

As a contribution to historical research, Arthur
Drews' work on early Christianity is worthless; as
a plea for the monistic faith which is to supplant
and embrace Christianity, it deserves more atten-

tion. As we have seen, many advocates of the theory, including Arthur Drews, W. B. Smith and K. C. Anderson, are concerned to promote the cause of true religion as they understand it. They hold that attachment to the historic Jesus is a positive degradation to true religion, or at any rate, a dangerous misunderstanding of the nature of true religion. Drews, at least, has all the fervour of an iconoclast. The *idea* of redemption is the great thing in Christianity, and each man must realize it for himself. To find God suffering in, and with, and for one's self is true religion. But this is simply obscured by the insistence on the need of a historic redeemer. To show that Jesus is but a symbol is, then, a great service to faith. The term "symbol" is the watchword of this whole movement. Dr. K. C. Anderson holds that the gospels are allegories after the pattern of Bunyan's *Pilgrim's Progress*. The story of the Virgin-birth enshrines the way in which truth comes to birth in the pure soul. Professor W. B. Smith has endeavoured to show that the miracles in Mark are as purely and as deliberately symbolical as the miracles in John. The whole tradition concerning Jesus has its value, not as a record of actual facts, but as a symbol of spiritual truths. The interpretations of the gospel narratives suggested by Smith and Anderson may be absurd and ill-founded, but the underlying theory is not so absurd, and is held by many who think them quite mistaken on the historical issue.

Ultimately the point before us is this, does symbolism provide an adequate account of the service of the figure of Jesus to religion? If it be maintained that the whole significance of Jesus is exhausted when we regard him as the symbol of certain eternal truths which yet are independent of him, then historicity matters little, and can never be a question of life and death for faith. Slight differences of opinion on this issue may be detected even where men are agreed in regarding Jesus as a symbol. It may be held with Drews that a symbol is more ideal and so more effective if it be divorced from history altogether. Or, following a more popular psychology, we may recognize that somehow the common people are more impressed by a symbol if it is a bit of real life and not pure allegory; and disregarding Drews' philosophic scorn of this weakness, we may admit that a fictitious Jesus, though still an effective symbol, and for the enlightened an equally effective symbol, would, as a matter of fact, lose influence among the masses of men. But on the whole the symbolists, if I may so call them, would maintain an attitude of indifference on this issue. Some may prefer a purely imaginary symbol; others advocate a historic Jesus, but all would say that in the end, the value of the symbol does not depend on historicity. A sentence or two from Mr. Lowes Dickinson puts the matter quite simply. " A man may, indeed, find a religious inspiration in the recorded life and sayings of Christ. But the inspiration would be the same whether he regarded the record of the gospels as myth or as fact, and would depend not on the existence of Christ in the past or in the present, but on the conception of life embodied in his story."

An essentially symbolist position was put before the religious Congress of Free Christians at Berlin in August 1911, by no less a scholar than Wilhelm Bousset. His paper fell into two parts: in the first, he dwelt on the difficulties of a historic basis for religious faith. He showed how difficult it was to determine exactly the teaching of Jesus, or to erect his teaching as it stands rooted in the culture of another age into a permanent authority. It is equally difficult to present a satisfying portrait of Jesus, to reach the secret of his inner life. Was not Wellhausen right when he said, we cannot disentangle the historic Jesus from the figure created by the Church's traditions? The second part of the paper was devoted to a positive theory of religion as based on reason rather than history. The part played by great personalities in developing religious ideas was frankly admitted, but after all, at the most they are symbols. "There is the culminating point of the affirmations permitted to us; images and symbols, symbols of a deeper reality, of an eternal truth, of this solid and permanent foundation which our anticipations grope after behind the symbols. Images, symbols, but not the ultimate truth." In these sentences, I believe, he was thinking primarily of the symbolic character of creeds, of affirmations concerning Jesus. But Jesus himself is a symbol, and the great advantage of this point of view is that it evades all the difficulties raised by historical criticism. The question of existence, of the historical attestation of facts no longer plays a predominant rôle: we are no longer obliged anxiously to separate in the portrait of Jesus elements which are perhaps added or created by the community from elements which are strictly historic.

163

We no longer have occasion to fear any possible result of research, since the exact truth remains for us, on many points, unknowable and for ever lost. What concerns us is the image, the symbol, not, in this matter, the truth, the ultimate reality. That abides behind the symbols, in the intangible reasons given by God to human reason, and in the eternal worth of the ideas. The symbol illustrates and explains, it does not prove. Hence note this curious point: the portrait of Jesus shown in the Gospels by his first disciples remains and will remain more effective as "poetry and truth" than all the attempts, however exact, to reconstruct his history. For faith is not concerned with historic reality in the narrow sense, but with the religious element. Faith dwells on the image, consciously or unconsciously. Words of Jesus, parables and writings, of which men can question the historic truth, can retain eternal worth. The fourth gospel, rejected by criticism, will never lose its religious power. And if science should pronounce the extreme verdict and say Jesus never existed, faith will not be lost, for faith rests on an eternal foundation of her own. Moreover, the portrait of Jesus in the gospels will endure as a poetic work if you will, but as poetry possessed of eternal symbolic worth.

This is the crucial passage, but it is necessary to supplement it by a few words on the general theory of religion which Bousset defends. He starts from Schleiermacher, and holds that religion is an essential element in human reason, that every man as such ought to find religion at the root of his being, as the fundamental and essential law of his life. Bousset was opposed to any idea of a supernatural revelation. Religion is not brought to man from without. It develops from within. "Religion is a primordial faculty of man which is only concerned to unfold itself in history, and which passes from its first obscure beginnings to an ever greater clearness. But history only develops that which existed from the beginning. That which existed originally passing through reflection, must reach a growing clearness in consciousness. This is a real progress." Furthermore, Bousset held that it must be possible to describe religion in a group of clear ideas. Indeed, the history of religion is the clarifying of certain ideas. These ideas are metaphysical or metascientific. There is the thought of the worth of life: the idea that the universe is not subject to chance but to necessity: the claim that the ultimate reality is spiritual and akin to ourselves: and a search for a supreme cause creative of liberty. Such ideas are not capable of scientific proof. Nor, indeed, can historic facts prove them. The old Rationalism was so far right in saying that eternal truths cannot be demonstrated by contingent historic incidents. But history still has a value. The historic process, the emergence of great figures which rivet popular attention and provide symbols of these great ideas, in which devotion can rest, makes easier the subjective appropriation of the truths of religion. Such thoughts as the purpose and worth of life and the spiritual nature of reality are not easy to grasp. Their strength lies without doubt in their own nature, but religion to become practically living must have symbols. Hence the rôle of great religious teachers in history. In this way Bousset finds a religious value in history, believes Jesus to be a historic figure and is glad of it, but in loyalty to his view of the nature of religion, he would have said with Schmiedel, " My inmost religious convictions would suffer no harm, even if I now felt obliged to conclude that Jesus never lived."[1]

This opens up a large field for discussion. The philosophy of religion implied in such a theory, in many ways resembles that adopted by Mr. Aldous Huxley in his most attractive book, *Ends and Means*. There he advocates a type of Hindu mysticism which is dangerously indifferent to history. In trying to determine the real importance of historic events, or rather of one historic person, we are really inquiring whether the liberal religious rationalism of Bousset and the philosophic mysticism of Aldous Huxley are adequate substitutes for the Christian gospel.

Before attempting to criticize, let me recapitulate the theory in brief. Religion consists essentially in ideas, ideas of a peculiar quality which belong to the human mind and unfold themselves in history. The development of such ideas is due to a succession of symbols, generally persons, which need not, however, be historic; and further, the origin and clarification of such ideas can be explained without the old-fashioned hypothesis of supernatural revelation. This last idea Bousset repudiates as vehemently as did Julian Huxley in a well-known work, and he must do so if he is to free religion from any final dependence on history. At the same time, it is difficult to see how we are justified in

[1] Schmiedel adds, " It would, of course, be a loss to me."

excluding the hypothesis of supernatural revelation, even in its crudest form of external communication. And I would be prepared to maintain that supernatural revelation is essential to religion. When Bousset speaks of religion as a primordial faculty of man, and says that history only develops that which existed from the beginning, and when, further, on the strength of this, he repudiates supernatural revelation, his account of religion in my judgment ignores its very essence. Of course if he includes God in that which exists from the beginning, the sentence is a truism, but in that case it is obvious that history may be made by supernatural revelation: it is not necessarily the unfolding of an original endowment of human nature if we once admit God. The only logical ground for excluding revelation would be to say, history merely unfolds that which was from the beginning in the human mind. But that is manifestly untrue, unless God be merely a part of human nature.

The story of religion can be nothing less than the self-communication of God to man, not merely the unfolding of a primordial faculty, though it is that, no doubt. And this self-communication may involve absolutely new developments in religious experience and conviction in the course of history, and such developments will be inseparably linked with particular events. Without pressing the bearing of this on historicity for the moment, I would reiterate that I see no attraction in this modern Deism, which pictures God as implanting in the human reason at the outset some intangible ideas which are left by

their inherent progressiveness to work themselves
unaided out of their primitive confusion into com-
parative clearness. Is there any evidence that
God has so treated us?

Even if we could allow that this story of
religious ideas justifiably excluded supernatural
revelation, is it in other respects a satisfactory
account of religion, and does it do justice to its
own admission that history is necessary to bring
clearness into this realm of thought? Does
religion consist primarily of ideas, and is the
relation of history to these ideas simply that of
symbol and reality? If religion be the inter-
relation of God and the soul, "the hiding and
seeking of Thee and me," then it may certainly
be described in a group of ideas; but its meaning
and context are never exhausted by ideas, unless
the term "idea" be redefined so as to avoid the
abstract intellectual character ordinarily associated
with it by the average man. But only if ideas are
regarded in this abstract fashion is it possible
to treat them as independent of their historical
expression. I can see that the truths of religion
must be super-historical, but can they be extra-
historical—can they be effectively dissociated from
the historical happenings, from the great figures
in history which we regard as their symbols?
Bousset's whole antithesis between history and
reason seems misleading and untenable. History
and reason are not alternative bases for religion;
they are mutually indispensable. Religion cannot
be based on reason apart from history, on the
simple ground that reason apart from history is
meaningless. I distrust the sharp distinction

168

which Bousset draws between the symbols and the eternal verities. Great religious teachers, he asserts, are symbols, images, but not the ultimate reality. As he handles the distinction it almost amounts to a separation. The symbols are more or less accidental, and I am only half reassured when the symbolic worth of Jesus is described as eternal. For if he, or any other symbol, be of eternal significance, then he must be more than a symbol. He is of the essence of the ultimate reality. Without him as its self-expression, not only would the ultimate reality not be known to us, but the ultimate reality would not be what it actually is. Philosophically there is perhaps no real distinction here. But since Bousset treats the historic symbols as of subsidiary importance, as merely a convenience for clearing up the ideas which in essence are independent of them, it seems worth while to press it.

The case I am trying to defend can appeal to the very nature of the ideas which *ex hypothesi* constitute religion. Bousset emphasizes as essential to religion, belief in the purpose and worth of life, belief in necessity rather than chance, belief that this necessity is reasonable and spiritual, akin to ourselves, and belief in a supreme spirit creative of liberty. We need not stop to inquire whether all these are intangible reasons bestowed by God on human reason as such; nor need we ask whether all religions could be brought within this group of ideas. For two consequences result from their vagueness: (1) It is precisely this quality that makes them seem independent of particular historic facts. Belief in *a* purpose for life, and in some sort of worth attaching to it, does not depend on any one symbol. Such belief, in various forms—divergent and conflicting forms—is yet a common factor in many religions, perhaps in all. (2) Again, it is precisely this quality of generality which shows that the fundamental ideas have not yet reached their necessary definiteness. The general human anticipation of a purpose in life, the general instinctive faith in the worth of life, are not established and justified until the true purpose is discovered, and that discovery must be associated with definite history. It is only by a process of sublimation that we turn Christianity into a system of ideas independent of history, and then we rob it of its true being. I can put my conviction most forcibly in this way. The essence of Christianity is not to be found in the Fatherhood of God and the Brotherhood of man, nor even in the truth " God is Love "; but rather in the assertion " God *so* loved the world." Christianity is not the association of God with love and fatherhood in general, but the definition of love and fatherhood by a particular act of God in history. Its message is not, " God is love and you can see this everywhere," but " God is love, for you cannot help seeing this in Jesus."

A closer connection between religious ideas and history than is recognized in Bousset's view may be admitted without thereby ascribing supreme importance to the historicity of Jesus. We must have history, and we have history of some sort in any case. If the Christ-myth theory were correct, Jesus himself would not be a historic figure, but the people in whose pious imagination the ideal-symbol took shape, would belong to the realm of history. Is not the one actuality as serviceable as the other? Do we need the historic Jesus, the actual deed, when we have the group inspired to think of God in this way?

If we were starting afresh, it is difficult to say how far a mythical Christ might help us. The myth of the dying and rising God undoubtedly influenced men to an extraordinary degree; and the purer morality, the more vivid imagination and intenser poetry of the story of Jesus might have rendered it profoundly moving, even if it were a myth and had been acknowledged to be myth from the first. But it is at least unfortunate that it was mistaken for history from the start, and that even on the showing of Drews and his co-workers, this very mistake was the foundation of its success. J. M. Robertson was not wrong in supposing that the whole case for treating religion as an illusion would be strengthened if Christ could be shown to be a myth. But apart from the particular circumstances of the rise of Christianity, which make it improbable that the gospel of love could be successfully replaced by "the sovereign legend of pity," it lies in the nature of the central Christian idea that only a historic figure can adequately represent it. The central idea, surely, is that God has visited and redeemed his people, fulfilled the Messianic promise in such sort that "when all was sin and shame, a second Adam to the fight, and to the rescue came." It would be a great thing if God inspired men to imagine so wonderfully what such a heaven-sent deliverer would say and do, but it could not fail to be a greater thing if such an one came in the flesh. So long as we are only in the realm of symbol, however inspired and inspiring, something is still wanting. God might do something more than he has yet done to reveal the greatness of his love towards us. If the Christ-myth be true, Christianity has only been conjectured, it is not created yet.

I do not see how a historic Jesus can fail to be a richer, fuller revelation of love than a myth, however beautiful. Put the case from the side of popular psychology. It is admitted by many that the sense of actuality influences men. Origen claims it as a mark of the humaneness of the gospel that the truth was presented in a person whom men could simply trust, and not in an argument which required philosophic training for its appreciation. I understand that to Hegel the truth of Christianity lies in the unity of man and God, a unity expressed in the historic incarnation which was needed to bring the truth home to unphilosophic, everyday humanity. I think Dr. McTaggart wrote of the Incarnation as a regrettable necessity from Hegel's point of view. Would it not cast a wonderful light on God's love that he apparently did not regret a necessity which seemed unfortunate to Hegel? Would it not commend God's love to us in that not only while we were yet sinners, but before we were metaphysicians, Christ died for us? There are verses in the Gîta in which Krishna, so to speak, excuses his human incarnations on the ground that his higher being is not affected thereby:

Misguided men despise Me when I enter into a mortal frame, not knowing My higher being as the great Lord of born beings. (lx. 11.)

Men of no understanding deem Me to have come from the unshown to the shown state, knowing not My higher being to be changeless, supreme. (vii. 24.)

We may contrast with these verses the line from the *Te Deum*, " When Thou tookest upon Thee to deliver man, Thou didst not abhor the Virgin's womb."

Is it not proof of the loftiness of the Christian thought of God's love that Christianity has never considered it necessary to offer the kind of apology for a historic incarnation which is found in the Gîta? Only in a man, and not in a myth, do we behold that condescension to the least, the lowliest and the lost, which is alone worthy of God.

CHAPTER XIV

WHAT DO WE KNOW OF JESUS?

IN this closing chapter I cannot do more than indicate an approach to an answer to our last question. It may be that even in Mark the element of interpretation is more pervasive and more distorting than we have hitherto supposed, and yet there are features of the record about Jesus of which the historic actuality and religious importance cannot be seriously questioned.

Within my life-time one of the happiest and most fruitful developments in the study of Christian origins has been the growth of better understanding and closer co-operation between Jewish and Christian scholars. Like the two parties of diggers engaged in making Hezekiah's tunnel in the Temple-area who could hear the sound of each other's picks, the scholars labouring on either side of a thin partition are growingly aware of one another's findings and begin to combine their efforts. Many have made notable contributions to this movement, but if any name be singled out for special honour, it must be that

of Claud Montefiore, who with such fairminded-
ness and such wealth of true scholarship has interpreted Jesus to his compatriots and Judaism to
Christians.

One main result of this development has been
to establish in detail the Jewishness of the gospels,
and indeed of Jesus himself. Henry J. Cadbury
in his stimulating Lowell lectures on *The Peril
of Modernizing Jesus*, rightly sums up the
position thus: "Taking the gospels at their face
value they attest what we should have expected
in advance from any early and trustworthy reports
of Jesus. His speech as quoted, his categories of
thought, his subjects of discussion, were all in the
manner and range of contemporary Judaism."
He adds: "In revealing the Jewishness of Jesus
the gospels supply at the same time credentials for
the general accuracy and contemporaneousness of
their own material." It is clear that the Jewish
background to the gospels presents insuperable
objections to any form of the Christ-myth so far
advanced. But this revelation of the Jewishness
of Jesus is important in other regards. It brings
home to us the sin and shame of the present-day
persecution of the Jewish people, at the hands of
governments which either actually call themselves
Christian or at least profess respect for positive
Christianity. If the link between Jesus and the
Jews were merely physical, if the whole truth of
the matter were comprised in Paul's phrase that
to the Jews belongs Christ according to the flesh,
since he is of the seed of David, born of a woman,
and born under the law, the barbarous treatment
of his brethren in Germany would remain a denial

of Christ as well as a degradation of German honour. But we are forced to recognize that there are closer ties between Jesus and his people. We tend to relate the teaching of Jesus to Judaism simply by contrasts, but he himself claimed to fulfil the law and the prophets, and in many of his teachings, he is in agreement with the best that is attributed to leading rabbis. These parallels from Jewish sources are often adduced to suggest that there is nothing original in the teaching of Jesus himself, or even that his teaching may be an artificial construct made by selection from Jewish ethical and religious precepts. But this is a misunderstanding of their real significance. The teaching of Jesus is not a cento of passages culled from any literary sources, and the originality of the teaching is not in the least impaired by the discovery of parallels. It is legitimate to recall the remark of Wellhausen who when it was claimed that all the leading sayings of Jesus might be found in the Talmud, observed: " Yes, and how much else! " The valid point brought out by the parallels is that there are genuine affinities between the teaching of Jesus and the outlook and wisdom of contemporary Judaism. This helps us to appreciate the profound truth of the saying of Claud Montefiore that " Jesus took the treasures of Israel and made them available for mankind."

Yet this could not be accomplished without applying a winnowing process to Judaism itself. If Judaism is rightly described as a national monotheism, there was bound to come a time when the truth of monotheism would burst the bonds of nationalism. At some time or other the overwhelming importance of the ethical religion of the prophets would be seen to outweigh the claims of ritual and tradition, especially the claims of such ritual and such tradition as merely serve to mark off Jew from Gentile. To introduce such a scale of spiritual values into the interpretation of the legacy of Israel could only be the work of an original mind, and the prophet who took the step would have to hazard his life. No leaderless group attributing their doctrines to a mythical Christ, would or could have issued such a challenge or effected such a change.

Now this or something like this is what Jesus actually did. He taught with authority. He believed himself to be loyal to the law, and yet he interpreted the law with a royal freedom. He treated the distinction between meats clean and unclean as of no religious value, and he regarded the law of Moses on the subject of divorce as a concession to human weakness rather than as an expression of the holy will of God. This was not Judaism as the Scribes understood it. The apprehensions of orthodox Jews were certainly intelligible. Nor were their apprehensions based only on the disregard of ritual purity in the use of foods. Jesus allowed unclean persons to touch him—the leper, for example, and the woman who was suffering from a hæmorrhage. Then he seemed to go out of his way to consort with disreputable persons—renegade Jews who collected taxes for alien rulers, and women who were known to be loose living. As Montefiore observes in his great commentary on the Synoptic Gospels,

M

" it is just here that opposition comes in and begins. To call sinners to repentance, to denounce vice generally, is one thing. To have intercourse with sinners and seek their conversion by countenancing them and comforting them—that is quite another thing. Did not all respectable persons pray and resolve to keep far from bad companions, to avoid the dwelling-place of the wicked? How can one keep the Law of God, if one associates with sinners? " Montefiore regards this as " a new original and historic feature " in the teaching of Jesus. We may add " a new original and historic feature in his conduct." The picture of Jesus as the friend of publicans and sinners is certainly drawn from the life.

In defence of his teaching and his conduct, Jesus could have appealed to the earlier prophets, particularly to Hosea and Jonah. But here a change had come over the spirit of Judaism, so that an appeal to the prophets seemed ineffective in the face of established law. Montefiore puts it thus, " When Amos and Hosea and Isaiah spoke, there was no universally recognized Divine and Mosaic Law. When Jesus spoke, there was. Hosea said, in God's name, ' I desire loving kindness and not sacrifices.' There was no possible retort—' But in the Law of God, which you, like everybody else, acknowledge to be perfect, immutable and divine, sacrifices are required in large numbers.' Jesus takes up the prophetic message under conditions which did not exist when the greatest of the Prophets declaimed their most specifically prophetic doctrine. The conflict—both the inward and the outward conflict—was therefore almost

178

inevitable."[1] Dr. Klausner, himself a keen Zionist, enables us to enter into the mind of patriotic religious leaders in Israel and to understand how dangerous the teaching and conduct of Jesus must have appeared in their eyes.

Judaism is a national life, a life which the national religion and human ethical principles (the ultimate object of every religion) embrace without engulfing. Jesus came and thrust aside all the requirements of the national life; it was not that he set them apart and relegated them to their separate sphere in the life of the nation: he ignored them completely; in their stead he set up nothing but an ethico-religious system bound up with his conception of the Godhead.

In the self-same moment he both annulled Judaism as the *life-force* of the Jewish nation, and also the nation itself as a nation. For a religion which possesses only a certain conception of God and a morality acceptable to *all* mankind, does not belong to any special nation, and, consciously or unconsciously, breaks down the barriers of nationality. This inevitably brought it to pass that his people, Israel, rejected him. In its deeper consciousness the nation felt that then, more than at any other time, they must not be swallowed up in the great cauldron of nations in the Roman Empire, which were decaying for lack of God and of social morality.

Israel's Prophets had taught that man was created in the image of God; they had proclaimed their message to all nations and kingdoms, and looked forward to a time when they would all call on the name of the Lord and worship him with one accord.

Israel's spiritual leaders, the Scribes and Pharisees, also looked for the time when " all creatures should

[1] C. G. Montefiore, *Some Elements of the Religious Teaching of Jesus*, p. 40 f.

179

fall down before one God " and all be made " one
society (a League of Nations) to do his will with a
perfect heart." And the people knew, if once they
compromised their nationality, that that ideal would
be left with none to uphold it, and that the vision
would never be fulfilled. Religion would be turned
to mere visionariness, and morality would be torn and
severed from life; while the manner of life of the
Gentiles, who were not yet capable of realizing such
an ethical standard, nor of being raised to the heights
of the great ideal, would remain more barbarous and
unholy than before.

Two thousand years of non-Jewish Christianity
have proved that the Jewish people did not err.[1]

This judgment raises many questions of absorb-
ing interest. Has Christianity been the complete
failure which Dr. Klausner suggests? And if in
Christian history there has been a tendency for
religion to become visionariness and for morality
to be divorced and torn from life, may it not be
that the failure of the majority of the Jewish people
to accept Jesus as the Christ has been in part the
cause? It is plausibly conjectured that Christianity
was too rapidly and too completely Hellenized
because Jewish Christianity was too weak numeri-
cally and too poor intellectually. But however
that may be, the judgment of Dr. Klausner is very
illuminating. It represents the frame of mind of
Saul of Tarsus as he journeyed to Damascus. And
it certainly represents truly the feeling of Scribe
and Pharisee as they listened with growing alarm
to what Jesus said and to what was said about him.
This conflict between Jesus and the religious

[1] *Jesus of Nazareth*, p. 390.

leaders of his people was a real conflict as it was a real tragedy. No evangelist imagined it, no group-consciousness projected it. No Jew ever wasted his breath denying the messiahship of a mythical Jesus. It was difficult for any Jews not to reject the claim to be Messiah, when it was made on behalf of an actual prophet who seemed to be annulling the life-force of the nation.

Closely bound up with this conflict and its outcome is another remarkable feature of the gospel records. In the gospels Jesus refers to himself as the Son of Man. The passages which seem to be most authentic fall into two groups. Some refer to the coming of the Son of Man, to his exaltation to the right hand of power, to his sitting on the throne of judgment. These witness to the final and enduring triumph of the Messiah. But others speak of the Son of Man being rejected and betrayed. These witness to his sufferings and death. The first type of saying is concerned with his *parousia*, i.e. his return in power and glory, while the second is concerned with his passion. The origin of the first group of sayings may be traced to the picture of the Son of Man, the heavenly Messiah, in the book of Enoch. But that the Son of Man must suffer many things *and be rejected of his people*—this doctrine is not clearly found in any apocalyptic writing or in any form of contemporary Judaism. It would seem that Jesus in referring to himself as Son of Man identified the glorious figure of the book of Enoch with the Suffering Servant in Isaiah liii. Such an identification, though it may be hinted at in one or two passages in Enoch, is most probably an original and historic feature in the teaching of Jesus. It determined his conception of his vocation and his destiny, and there can be little doubt that he was led to associate Messiahship with suffering because he was aware of the gulf that was opening out between himself and his people.

The belief that the idea of a suffering Messiah is derived directly from Isaiah liii. is erroneous. Some rabbis appear to have given a Messianic interpretation to the greatest of the Servant prophecies at least in part. They thought the Messiah might suffer but did not expect him to die for the sins of the people.[1] Nor is the conception of a suffering Messiah to be found in the expectation of a second subsidiary Messiah, a Messiah Ben-Joseph who was to die in battle for his people. This Messiah Jesus refused to be, and in any case, Messiah Ben-Joseph was not identified with the suffering servant of Isaiah liii, and no atoning significance was attributed to his death. The reasonable conclusion is that Jesus himself made the identification of the heavenly Son of Man with the suffering servant. He came to believe that he was to be rejected by his people, that he must die and that his death would have the redeeming efficacy of that of the man of sorrows, acquainted with grief.

Those, however, who think that this is primitive Christian doctrine and interpretation rather than Jesus's self-description, will be constrained to admit that this interpretation of Isaiah liii. is inspired by the historic fact of the crucifixion and

[1] See Abrahams in *The People and the Book*, pp. 408-10; and Strack-Billerbeck, II, p. 282 f.

that the fact of the crucifixion cannot be a mere deduction from the prophecy. There is a revealing passage in Justin's dialogue with his Jewish friend, Trypho. At one stage, when Justin appeals to Isaiah liii, Trypho is prepared to admit that this passage might refer to the Messiah. The Messiah might conceivably suffer and even die for the sins of the people. But, he hastens to add, I cannot believe that he would die on a cross—a shameful death which is under a curse in the Law. No Jew would ever have imagined crucifixion as the fate of the Messiah.[1] To suggest, as Dr. Couchoud does, that Paul introduced the cross into Christianity is ridiculous. Paul never invented the cross. He stumbled over it as his compatriots did, before ever he preached it. As we have seen, there is no sign anywhere of crucifixion as a mode of human sacrifice, and among Jews such a sacrificial ritual would have been impossible. There is no accounting for the story of the Cross, except that it happened so. This was, in fact, the outcome of the historic conflict between Jesus and his own people.

Perhaps it was not the outcome which Jesus anticipated, as it was certainly not the outcome he desired. The predictions of the passion in the gospels are quite possibly coloured in detail by the actual event, and Rudolf Otto has suggested that if Jesus spoke more vaguely of being rejected by his people, he may have anticipated death by stoning, as happened to Stephen. In this case, the way of the cross only became clear and certain to him at the last. But this is only a conjecture. What is clear is this, that crucifixion was a Roman punish-

[1] Justin, *Dial. cum Tryphone*, c. 32 and c. 89-90.

ment, and that the Roman state shares the moral responsibility for the crucifixion along with the Jewish church. No Christian group invented this. The fiction would have served no Christian end. A Christian invention would have thrown all the blame on the Jews. "Suffered under Pontius Pilate" is undeniable historic fact.

Whether we believe it or not, whether we like it or not, Christ died for us. He died, not to purchase pardon from an angry God, but to save his people from their sins and to save us from our sins. It has been well said that the death of Socrates stopped, or at least stemmed, the moral rot in Greece. Socrates died to convince men that truth is not a mirage and justice not a cloak to self-interest, but that truth and justice are realities for which a man may gladly give his life. So the death of Christ stands as a barrier between mankind and moral decadence. Christ died to convince us that God is not just an impersonal reality of which we may be aware in moments of mystic exaltation, but one who cares for the least of his creatures and whose love desires not the death of a sinner but rather that he turn from his wickedness and live. Christ died to convince us that love to God and love to our neighbours are our highest loyalties. Christ died to challenge our moral cowardice and to undermine our self-complacency and pride. Christ died to convince us of the miracle of forgiveness and to save us from sinking as we are sinking now into barbarism and secularism. In short, Christ died to make us good.

Christ may have been mistaken. He may have been mistaken about God. He may have been mistaken as to the necessity and purpose of his own death. But there at long last is the strange man on a cross—no myth, no phantom, but a man like and unlike ourselves. Try as we may, we cannot get him out of history, and if we have any sense for reality, we cannot evade his challenge. Christ may have been mistaken, but was he? He may have died for nothing, but did he?

INDEX

187

Index

189

Index

Index

191

Index